Playing with Anxiety:
Casey's Guide for Teens & Kids

Reid Wilson, PhD and Lynn Lyons, LICSW

To receive updates and new support materials for this book, register at *www.playingwithanxiety.com*

ISBN 978-0-9630683-3-0

This is a companion book to *Anxious Kids, Anxious Parents: Seven Ways to Stop the Worry Cycle and Raise Courageous and Independent Children*, by Reid Wilson, PhD and Lynn Lyons, LICSW (HCI Books, 2013).

Cover design and book layout by
Red Nebula, Inc. · RedNebulaInc@gmail.com

Drawings by
Sumanta Baruah · sumanta.baruah@gmail.com

Solving the Worry Puzzle

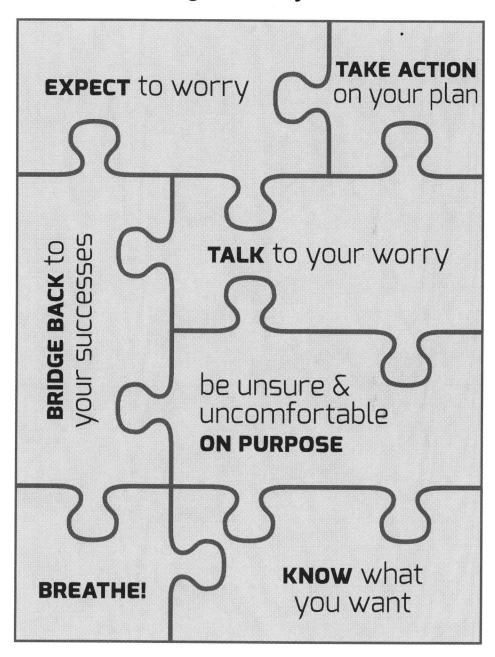

EXPECT to worry

TAKE ACTION on your plan

BRIDGE BACK to your successes

TALK to your worry

be unsure & uncomfortable **ON PURPOSE**

BREATHE!

KNOW what you want

Playing with Anxiety:
Casey's Guide for Teens and Kids

Table of Contents

Introducing Myself

Let's see if we have anything in common. I'm Casey, and I'm a kid who knows worry. I know dread, too. And I've learned some great tricks about how to get out of things. And some not-so-great tricks... (Do you know that by holding a thermometer over a match flame, you can get the temperature up to 108 degrees? And then the tip turns black and melts a little.)

How about you? Are you a kid who relates to what I'm saying? This book is for you.

I'm a lot better now. I've got control of my worry and pretty good control of my anxiety. I didn't take a magic pill, so if you are looking for that you can stop reading now. But I did learn about what I was doing wrong. Lots! And that's fine because that's what worry does: it gets you way off track.

I also figured out how to get back on the right track (after lots of good, hard work). You won't have to work as hard as I did because I'm going to give you the answers. Don't let that concern you; this isn't a test, so I can pass along my solutions. I'll help you understand what's going on in your body, share some very cool tricks and gimmicks, tell you stories about how I got better, and about how my friend Shannon, and my brother, Elliot, became our guinea pigs. They got over some big fears, too. Although Elliot says the success was mostly him, with just a little coaching from me.

As luck would have it, Mom and I worked this stuff out together. (By the way, I wasn't alone in the mistakes category. Mom was making plenty, too.) So if you are a parent of a kid who stays away from anything new and scary, this book is for you, too. But I'm writing it to help kids, OK? I'm not that good at fixing parents.

Chapter 1: A Glob of Caterpillars

I'm familiar with the computer at my house, and it generally behaves like I want it to. I know how to surf the net and play games and watch videos. I can download music or movies, and find stuff on line for school and for fun. But do I understand how that thing *works*? No way. When it breaks, can I fix it? Absolutely not! My cousin is a computer technician. He fixes computers and sets up systems for big companies. He tried to explain some of his job to me once, and I was lost within the first two minutes. (I kept nodding in agreement and saying, "Really?" so he wouldn't think I was less-than-smart.)

Mom says it's the same with cars. She's familiar with the basics of our car, like the difference between the gas and brake pedals, and how to check the oil. But could she explain to me how the engine works? Does she understand what happens under the hood? "Casey," she'd say, "That's a mystery to me."

Pull Your *Back* Brakes First!

Do you have a bike with hand brakes? Have you ever been riding along and then pulled hard on your front brakes? Don't try it! You'll flip right over your handlebars! Yes, I did. Cracking my helmet on the asphalt sure motivated me to *understand* what my brakes can do. Now

I'm clear that when I'm going fast and I pull on my front brakes, I can stop my front wheel from spinning. But the rest of the bike, and my body, will keep moving forward, right on past that stationary front wheel. (In physics they call it inertia.)

Since that little unexpected meeting between my head and the road, I've followed that brake cable line with my finger and my eyes, all the way from the handle to the brake pads on my front wheel. I've squeezed the front brake handle and watched those brake pads press against the rim of the wheel. My friend Sylvia held the front of the bike up while I spun the wheel and then squeezed the front brake. I've ridden my bike slowly, and then jammed on the front brake to feel the back end of the bike lift a bit off the ground. (Now *that* you can try.)

After checking all that out, I now understand how the brakes on my bike work. When I didn't know this stuff, I ended up hurting myself. It's unfortunate I had to get hurt to learn the lesson, but it was, without a doubt, worth learning.

So, you might ask, what does this have to do with being worried and scared? I'll tell you: it's the difference between being familiar with something, and understanding something. If you're reading this book, you already know what it's like it's like when you're scared. You know the way it feels in your body. I'll bet you're pretty familiar with worry, too. I'm guessing you think about it a lot. My worries took up far too much of my time and energy. I felt like worry was my companion, whether I liked it or not. I was totally and completely *familiar* with worry. We hung out together. But even after spending so much time together…

Did I really understand worry?

Did I know how it worked? Why it was there? What to do about it?

Did I have a clue about what was happening in my body and in my mind?

Could I keep it from getting stronger or taking control of my life?

The feelings and sensations of being worried and scared where so powerful and familiar, but did I really *get it*?

NO. Capital-N, capital-O. NO. I knew how I felt when I worried, but much of worry was a mystery to me. A confusing, frustrating mystery.

Well, now I know how worry works. It's not that mysterious to me anymore. It actually makes a lot of sense. Do you remember when I introduced myself I told you how I have done a lot of the work for you already? I talked about how Mom and I worked together to figure this stuff out. You're not going to have to work that hard to figure things out, because I'm going to help you solve the mystery, right from the start.

Yes, I know you're already familiar with worry. But you don't understand it.

"So, you're saying that being familiar is different than understanding?" you ask.

Yes, it is, and I'll explain. (That's why we're here, after all. And you catch on fast.)

It's like your computer or your family car. You know how worry makes you feel—do you ever!—but you can't explain how it operates, can you? You're familiar with it, but you don't understand it. In this book we're shooting for understanding.

I got hurt on my bike, and that motivated me to figure out how my bike works. I could have quit riding, and then I wouldn't get hurt again. But I *want* the adventures that riding gives me, so I learned to handle my brakes. **Worry has hurt me**, and that has motivated me to **figure out how worry works**. For a while, I quit doing the things that I worried about. Then I didn't worry so much. But I *wanted* those adventures back in my life. So I learned to handle worry. For me, learning and understanding felt like a deep, satisfying breath. And here's the good news: understanding worry is so much easier than understanding how computers work!

But I'm jumping ahead, so let's back up to how Mom and I figured all this stuff out. My problems with worry sort of snuck up on us. Looking back on it, I certainly had some anxieties before kindergarten, but I don't even think my mom and I used the words "worry" or "problem" when I was five or six or seven. I was afraid of birthday parties, so my mom stayed at the parties with me. We skipped the Fourth of July fireworks at the park each summer. If we went to the movies, we sat in the aisle seats in case I wanted to leave. We thought we were just being careful. We even thought we were **smart**, because all of our planning kept me from crying, shaking, and yelling. Mission accomplished. No problem.

Then came second grade. Mom had to beg me to get out of bed in the mornings, and I cried when it was time to leave for the bus. So Mom let me skip the bus, and she drove me. But then I refused to get out of the car when we pulled up to the front of the school. The teacher came to get me, and I cried and yelled and begged. I complained of tummy aches, and the nurse was always calling Mom to pick me up. (I told the nurse I was going to throw up, so who can blame her?)

Mom tried to follow our plan of being careful and keeping me calm. She didn't make me take the bus. She walked me into school and told the nurse she'd come get me right away if I was feeling "sick." She gave me those chalky tablets that grown-ups take for stomach aches and took me to the pediatrician a few times to make sure nothing was wrong with my stomach. None of it helped. I started missing more and more school. When I did go, I was behind the other kids in math and spelling, so of course that made me feel worse. Honestly, almost **everything** we were doing made matters worse, but back then we had no idea. Did you know there are certain types of fires—grease fires, they're called—that actually get worse when you throw water on them? If you're in the kitchen and cooking bacon, and the grease catches on fire, water actually makes the fire bigger! Mom thought she was helping, and I wanted to feel better, but we were making the worry bigger. Like throwing water on a grease fire, it seemed like the right thing to do, but it wasn't.

We were familiar with worry, but we didn't understand it. We kept trying, but we weren't fixing anything. I refused to do lots of different activities. Avoiding things made me kind of comfortable, and we accepted that as good enough. For a while, anyway. Until my holiday recital at school in fourth grade.

We were getting ready to go to school for the recital. I had three songs to sing with the chorus, and my class had decorated the gym with paper snowflakes that afternoon. I was wearing my new green dress, and Mom and I were sitting on the bed while she put my hair into a special braid. I did feel nervous, but I really—and I mean *really*—wanted to go. Plus, after the recital, my friends and I were planning to go out for ice cream with our families. Who wants to miss that!

But suddenly, as Mom was braiding my hair, I threw up. All over my dress. I'd never done that before. I often felt sick to my stomach, and I hardly ever ate breakfast before school, but I'd never actually **puked**. There I was, sitting on the bed, covered in throw up. I cried. Mom cried. Elliot came running into the bedroom and stood there looking at us, not saying a word. We didn't go the concert. My mom said I could wear my blue dress with the black buttons, but I was too upset. She even offered to take me to meet my friends for ice cream after the concert. I just couldn't do it. She cleaned me up, and she cleaned up the mess, too. That night I cried myself to sleep.

Okay, I know that sounds like a sad story, but that night changed everything. The next morning we began to talk about missing the recital, and we both started crying again. This worry stuff was running my life. When I first started to worry, avoiding things made me feel better. Now worry and avoiding meant missing out on fun stuff, like recitals and ice cream. And important stuff, like learning to read chapter books.

As we talked, our tears stopped. And we both started to get mad. We decided then and there that we were going to treat this worry thing as a puzzle. And we were going to solve it! We didn't even know what the pieces of the puzzle looked like, much less how to put them together. But at that moment we committed ourselves to putting together the puzzle. We hooked our pinkies, and made an unbreakable pinkie promise: we would not stop until we fixed my worry problem. Then we all went out for pancakes. It was a little too early for ice cream.

I won't tell you everything we did, because it involved thinking and talking and reading and writing and interviewing, over and over again, for a good long time. If I told you about all that, you'd get bored and quit reading, and that would defeat the purpose of all our hard work. So give me credit for two things: how much work I did for you, and how you only have to hear about the highlights.

Boo Runs Scared

I have a cat named Boo. He's an average cat. He's black and white, and he's fairly lazy most of the time. Last summer, a dog wandered into our yard. Actually, he looked like he was there for a purpose. He was a big brown bloodhound with long droopy ears and a wrinkled face, sniffing along, following his nose right up our driveway to the front porch. Boo was napping there in the sun. He must have heard the dog coming, because he opened his eyes just as the dog's nose arrived at the first porch step.

Boo jumped up. His back arched, and he seemed to be standing on his tippy toes. His tail fluffed out like a feather duster. His ears flattened back on his head, and he made **the most amazing growling noise** from deep in his throat. I'm sure his heart was pounding and his pupils were so big his entire eyes looked black.

I opened the door, and Boo came tearing into the house as I shooed the dog away (even though he seemed quite friendly). Once Boo was in the house and feeling safe, he began to calm down. His fur and eyes and ears returned to normal. The poor cat was so scared outside, facing what seemed to be a terrifying predator. But within a few minutes inside, he was napping under the couch.

I sat down, cocked my head, and stared at the sleeping cat. Those little cogs started turning around in my brain. Hmmm. Boo was scared. And this fear helped him get away from the dog. And now he's done with it all and comfortably settled under the couch.

Suddenly, my heart started racing and my hands got instantly clammy. I felt an urge to get up and run, and I had no idea why. Until, that is, I paid attention to what had just popped up in my mind. Watching Boo's episode triggered a memory of my *own* encounter with a dog, and I was reliving it right at that moment. Let me tell you about it. (If I was a movie director, this is where I'd yell, "Cue flashback music!")

I'm not generally afraid of dogs. I like them. Lots of my family members have dogs, so I'm around them a bunch. But on my way to the school bus stop one day, I heard this loud, aggressive barking that seemed to be coming right at me. Suddenly I see a dog as big as *me*, coming right *at* me, with her lips curled up and her long sharp fangs showing, and her jaw opening and snapping shut, again and again. I screamed and ran as fast as my legs would take me. That dog's owner had tied her around a thick tree with a thick chain, and there was no way she could get to me behind that chain-linked fence. But in that moment, I didn't have that information, and I was literally running for my life.

Once I got past the yard, and she quieted down, I was so relieved. But my heart was pounding out of my chest, and I didn't really settle down for another hour. (So don't ask me what we talked about in social studies class; I wasn't paying much attention.) I learned my lesson that day. Now when I get close to her yard, I cross to the other side of the street. What's the lesson? It's not that the dog is dangerous. After all, she's tied up and behind a fence. The lesson is that if I don't want to see and hear her aggressive charge toward me, I can cross the street. **That's smart, don't you think?**

Wow, I'm experiencing something interesting. Even right now, as I'm writing this to you a year after that scary event, I can still imagine that dog coming toward me at lightning speed, and I can hear her hostile barks. My heart is speeding up again, just like it did when I was staring at Boo under the couch. But I'm OK with that, because now I know that it's normal to get scared just *thinking* about a scary event. It happens to everybody. And I expect it to happen again. Even though I get uncomfortable, I know it's my body and mind's way of protecting me. You'll see.

Be Afraid—Be Very Afraid

Remember how I cocked my head to the side while I stared at Boo, then had that scary image of the dog coming toward me? Well, a couple of moments later—while my heart was revving like a race car engine at the starting line—I thought, "Boo and I have something in common. The same thing seemed to help *both* of us. Really? The cat and I both act the same when we're scared? **Are we *supposed* to worry?**"

Mom and I did a lot of studying and asking questions to find out if I was on the right track. What did we discover? Worry is normal, and sometimes it can be helpful. I need it, you need it, everybody we know needs it. Including Boo and all of the other mammals on Earth. Everybody worries! Everyone *must* worry! You're not going to get completely rid of it *ever* (if you know what's good for you.)

I know this might sound strange to you. "Worry is helpful? Then how come grown-ups tell me to stop worrying, or that there's nothing to be afraid of?" I said it's normal and *sometimes* helpful. Worry can help you, and it can also hurt you. You're going to learn that difference in this book. Keep reading and you'll see.

You can't get rid of all your scared feelings. Sorry. I know that disappoints you. But it's actually good news, because when we are afraid, we...

...**STOP** when it's smart to think about what we're about to do

...**BACK AWAY** from things when it's smart to avoid

...**RUN AWAY or fight** when the danger is real

Let's look at these three benefits of getting scared. When we're learning something new, like how to ride a bike on the street or how to swim in the deep end of the pool without a noodle, it's smart to have a little voice inside that says, "Hey, stop for a moment. You're still learning. Remember your skills before you go forward again." My fifth grade teacher called it "Good Judgment Juice," and he said we could all use a dose now and then.

There's a show on television (Mom doesn't let us watch it, but I saw it at my friend's house once) where these guys do crazy, stupid things and usually get hurt. Maybe you've seen it. I used to think I was such a coward, and I wished that I could be like them, and never feel scared or worried. But now when I think about that show, I understand that when I'm afraid in some situations, I stop. I don't do stupid or unsafe things. I'm not a coward; I'm smart!

Grown-ups say, "There's nothing to be afraid of," because they're trying to make us feel better. But that advice is not always true. We're **smart to feel afraid** sometimes. It's a natural response in ALL of us. When we hear, "STOP!" in our mind, **sometimes we should listen**.

(Now, for you worriers: there is such a thing as being afraid *too* much...but you already know that, don't you? We'll talk later about what to do when you're afraid too often. Keep reading!)

In addition to slowing us down, feeling scared can help us **back away** from things that we should avoid. You know how when you go to the movies, they show the previews of coming attractions (called "trailers")? Sometimes I watch a preview that looks great. "I want to see that movie," I think to myself. Sometimes, though, they show one that is scary or way too violent. When that happens, I close my eyes and plug my ears. I fidget around in my seat. My heart starts to speed up a bit. Just from watching the preview! So I skip that movie when it comes to the theater. Also smart, right?

Here's that third good reason for feeling scared. **It helps you run away** if there is a real danger. That brings us back to the story about Boo last summer. That dog was a real danger to him—he didn't know the dog, the dog was bigger than he was, and of course there's that whole dog-versus-cat thing that has existed for all time—so **being afraid got him ready** to protect himself in a flash.

I had just had my own kid-versus-dog thing that spring, so I knew, as I stood there, exactly what was going on with Boo. I watched it happening, and so I understood it immediately. That was **fear at its finest moment!** It happens to all animals (including us humans) when we feel threatened or think we're in danger. They call it the fight-or-flight response, and it's amazing! When Boo saw that big strange dog, his body jumped into action. It prepared him to *fight* if the dog came closer, or to take *flight* (which means get away quickly) if the opportunity was there. As I opened the door, smart Boo chose flight, and ran to safety inside.

When I saw that dog—as big as *me*—coming at me, running and barking, my legs just started moving on their own. They shifted gears from walk to fly-like-the-wind in no seconds flat. I couldn't have been happier that my feet knew what to do so quickly, so automatically. Because at that moment I was thinking, "Oh, no! Here comes something awful!" I wasn't thinking of how to protect myself.

That was *my* fight-or-flight response, too. When we feel scared or threatened, it's normal for our body to do take actions that protect us. If you're going to solve this mystery of worry, you must absorb this piece of very important information: your body has a fear response, and physical things happen in your body during that response. Evolution designed it that way, and **it comes in handy** sometimes.

Look what it did for Boo:
- His fur puffed out and his back arched. That's so he'd look bigger and more threatening to his enemy, the dog.
- His pupils dilated (that means got bigger) so he could see well.
- He growled and hissed, to let that dog know he meant business.
- His heart pounded, so blood could carry oxygen to his muscles faster, so he could…
- Run away quickly!

Now, a human's fight-or-flight response is a bit different (no fur, no tail), but the purpose is the same: to **get you ready for action**. It's been the same since caveperson times, when we had to run away from saber-toothed tigers and other big creatures.

Look what I did:

Basically, I ran-like-the-wind.

Boo and I did most of the same things when we sensed danger. And so do you.

When you feel scared, **here's what usually happens**:
- Your brain signals your body to release special chemicals, like adrenaline [uh-dren'-uh-lin]. (You don't have to remember that word, but it can make you sound like an expert if you do). They

signal your body to get ready to run away or stay to protect yourself.

- Your heart starts to beat faster (to get that blood and oxygen to your big muscles).
- You breathe faster, almost like a dog panting (without the tongue hanging out). This gives your muscles more oxygen in case you need to work hard. And it gives your brain more oxygen in case you have to think more creatively.
- You start to sweat. This is how your body cools you down, so you don't get overheated. I also read that sweating makes your skin **slippery, so you can escape** from your enemy. How clever is that!
- The pupils in your eyes (the black part) get bigger, like Boo's, so you can see better.
- Your stomach might feel strange. This is because your body doesn't pay any attention to digesting food when it's in danger. It's paying attention to those **big, helpful, getting-away muscles**.

Spray, Slap, and Play Dead

By the way, right now you may be thinking, "Wow, Casey is super-smart to figure all this stuff out." Here's a reminder: I didn't figure it out myself. Lots of people, especially Mom, helped me find this stuff. We read books and talked to people. It took us a long time to solve the puzzle, to start winning at this game. Aren't you glad I'm your coach and can show you the shortcuts? (You're welcome.)

When I learned this stuff, I was impressed. I studied animals in nature, and what they do to protect themselves. Skunks spray stinky stuff (avoid them, okay?), **beavers slap their tails** on the water to warn of danger, dogs growl and show their teeth (boy, do they!), chipmunks and mice freeze like statues or run into tiny spaces, and possums play dead (which I think is quite ingenious.) That's why we *could* call this the fight-flight-or-freeze response. Do you ever "freeze up" when the teacher calls on you for an answer, and you weren't really listening, so you're not sure what to say?

In the Amazon jungle, the lowly caterpillars, who are only about two inches long, group together in the hundreds on the side of a tree so that they look like one very big unappealing glob of green. That's so the birds don't see them as tasty little nutritious morsels, and they leave them alone. And how about the Zebras in Africa? I always thought it was strange that black and white stripes covered their bodies. How do they protect themselves from predators (the animals who want to eat them) when they can't blend into the brown surroundings of the African savannah? Well... **a dazzle of Zebra** (that's what they call a herd) runs zigzag together as they are escaping. This creates an optical illusion (a false image), so predators can't track one animal well enough to attack it. By the way, here's another cool thing about Zebras: babies are born with legs as long as the adults are. So when they mix in with the herd during the weeks after their birth, they stand as tall as the adults. Then the predators can't spot their little bodies in the crowd.

What's Next?

Honestly, I could go on and on about the very cool ways that animals protect themselves from danger. (I heard about this octopus that **changes** its skin—I mean actually changes it—to match its environment!) But I think I've made my point. All creatures, including humans, need to sense danger at times, and have developed protective responses that help keep them alive and safe. And that's a good thing. However... (you could sense that was coming, couldn't you?) ...now we need to start talking about being *too* afraid and how those fears and worries switch from helpful and clever, into uncomfortable and annoying.

Next stop? Your genes, your temperament, and your busy life. I, your coach, and Chapter 2 await you.

Chapter 2: Don't Climb That Tree!

The O'Donnell family—three boys and a girl—lives a few houses away from us. All four kids have red hair and these ears that stick out a bit. (Not that there's anything wrong with that.) They have freckles and brownish eyes. In the summer, you can see their ribs when they wear bathing suits. The dad is a taller version of the kids, except I can see some grayish hair mixed in with the red.

My brother and I don't match up like that at all. Our hair and eyes and bodies are really different from each other. Most people wouldn't even guess we're related.

This has to do with genes. Genes are the pieces of information that come together and begin to make you who you are. They can influence how a person looks, or how a person reacts to certain situations. You get some from your mom's side, and some from your dad's, and they are put together **like a jigsaw puzzle**. Many combinations of genes are possible —like a build-your-own-sundae bar with eighty bazillion different ingredients—so sometimes people in families look alike, and sometimes they look very different. Genes can also influence things we can't see right away, like allergies to strawberries, or a talent for music.

Mom and I started out hoping to find THE answer to why I kept getting so scared about different things. If we could find that ONE answer, we thought we could beat my worries like superheroes defeating a villain. That's why Mom and I read a lot about genes and worry. We were hoping that "genes" would be that ONE answer. (It isn't. No big surprise.)

The truth is this: kids get scared and start worrying for all sorts of reasons. You just learned some of the helpful ones: we slow down when it's smart to take our time, we avoid things when it's smart to back away, and we run away when the danger is real. Worry can even give us a signal that we have too many tasks piling up or too many distractions bothering us. But how about these not-so-helpful worries? Why do *they* show up? How do they get stronger? That's what we'll talk about now.

This information has the potential to bum you out. You might start imagining how bad things can get or think that this is too big a problem to fix. It's like the nurse telling you all the ways you can catch a cold, or the teacher reviewing all the mistakes you keep making on your tests. I certainly don't want you to get discouraged while you're learning about worry. So here is an important tip. This tip might help you feel a little less worried as you read this stuff. Hard to say, really.

The tip? These not-so-helpful worries can seem like some sneaky trickster, hard to capture and harder to tame. But they **aren't as tricky as they seem** to you right now. Once they take over, they get less clever. So that means fixing your worries is not complicated. You'll have to work, but it's not complex work, especially when you have a plan. My plan works, and it can help you with all different types of not-so-helpful worries. Do you hear me? Nod if you hear me. Good.

Wearing Your Genes

Let's get back to this gene stuff, which can get really complicated. Some researchers spend their whole lives trying to figure it out. Luckily, you have me!

Mom and I found out that genes can influence how much a person worries, even the not-so-helpful variety: the kind that get in our way and make us too uncomfortable. Annoying, to say the least. And at their worst? They make us think *way* too much, and convince us to back away from activities.

When I was younger I had a friend named Lizzie. We had a lot of fun together, but we always played at her house, and she really didn't talk much, especially to grown-ups. (I guess I talked enough for the both of us!) But I never quite understood why she acted that way. Then, as I was learning about all this stuff, it became a lot clearer. Scientists are certain that if a little kid is **very shy**, even as a toddler (two or three years old), then that kid is **more likely to be a worrier** as she gets older. These kids might have trouble letting go of their parent's leg at the playground, and don't want to be left with a babysitter. Maybe they cry more often, and aren't excited about going to preschool. Sometimes these shy kids are really quiet, too. And that sounded like Lizzie!

This doesn't mean that *all* shy little kids grow up to be worriers. It just means there's a connection between these two things. And a pretty good one. The worry researchers call it a "greater likelihood." If you're a very shy kid, there's a greater likelihood you'll be a worrier as you get older, but there are things you can do that make the worrying better or worse. It's like taking care of your teeth. If you brush and floss, there's no *guarantee* you'll be cavity-free, but your chances are much better. And if you don't brush them, there's no guarantee you <u>will</u> get cavities, but there's a "greater likelihood" you will.

A chance. A likelihood. Not a certainty. A chance.

Remember how I'm going to give you a plan? If you're a shy kid, you need a plan. It's like **brushing and flossing your brain.** Learning the plan and using the plan is just like creating another good habit. And—hello—you're not going to *really* brush and floss your brain. That's gross.

Mom Decides to Change Her Ways

When Mom and I learned that "worry genes" were not going to explain, completely, why I was a worrier (I wasn't even one of those shy little kids, by the way), we felt good and bad at the same time. We felt good because I didn't have some part of me that guaranteed I'd be a worrier. And neither do you! Before we did our research, we thought maybe that was the case. No. My eye color is permanent and unchangeable. Being a worrier can be **temporary and changeable**. We were happy to discover that.

But we felt bad—well, when I say "we" I mean mostly Mom— because Mom began to realize that maybe the worrying was passed down from parent to child, but not in just a genetic way. Maybe she was SHOWING me how to be a worrier. Maybe she was **teaching me without knowing it**. Ouch. That was a tough one for her.

Mom was determined to reverse whatever she was doing that might be showing me and my brother how to be worried. She read books and looked at research. She talked to an expert on families and parenting and worry. She learned some important stuff, and she wants me to share them with you and your parents. Your parents should read this book, and they should absolutely read this part. Tell them it's full of "essential information." That phrase usually gets a parent's attention. But try not to say, "This is all *your* fault." They tend to stop listening then.

Without knowing it, parents can help worry show up and even make it stronger. How? Two ways:

- *They* might be worriers.
- They want to make their kids feel better.

Let's start with the first one. **Parents might be worriers**, and this helps worry show up in kids. Parents teach us things. We learn to speak their language, to put our shoes on, to use the toilet. They show us how to hit a baseball, the way to cut our meat, and where to go on the first day of school. In the olden days, parents taught their kids their future jobs. Farmers trained little farmers, and blacksmiths trained little blacksmiths. Women taught their daughters to bake and to mend socks. (Things were different for girls back then. Not a lot of options for us.) Have you ever heard that expression, "Like father, like son?" Or "Like mother, like daughter?" It's been around forever.

Parents generally teach what they know. So it makes sense that if one of your parents tends to worry, then that parent may accidentally teach you to worry in the not-so-helpful way. I don't think for a minute that Mom sat down one day when I was a little kid and figured out how to make me worry too much. According to her, she didn't even *know* she was worrying so much. She was simply telling me to watch where I walked, to chew my food so I didn't choke, and to stay out of the deep end of the pool so I wouldn't drown. Solid advice, if you ask me.

Mom and I learned, though, that **worried grown-ups** often **parent** a bit **differently** than non-worried grown-ups. At the park the other day, we listened to a mom talk to her son. She was pushing him on the swing, and she told him over and over and OVER again to hold on tight. He wanted to go down the slide, but she said it was too dangerous. "You might hit your head, or knock your teeth out!" Boy, after listening to her, I didn't want to go down the slide either!

As we talked about it later, Mom remembered an example of teaching me to be scared at the park, way back when I was seven. I was just getting my leg up around the first branch of this great climbing tree. She remembers yelling out, "Don't climb up in that tree, Casey! You might fall out and break your neck!" OK… so… if *she* was scared, she could come over and teach me how to climb safely. And if she wanted to scare *me*, couldn't she have said, "You might break your arm"? Did she have to say, "You might break your *neck*"? I can handle breaking my arm. I wouldn't want to have to handle breaking my neck. So Mom realized that she was making me *too* scared by saying that.

Parents need to offer directions and help, but sometimes the help ends up making us *more* afraid. Parents need to keep kids safe, but worried parents might have a hard time knowing when safe is safe enough.

Then there's the second way that parents help worry show up or get stronger: they want to make their children feel better. Parents are *supposed* to make their kids feel better, aren't they? They don't want their kids to stay scared or uncomfortable. Pretty much every day since I was born, Mom feeds me, makes sure I'm warm, takes care of me when I'm sick, packs my lunch, checks my seatbelt, tucks me in.... you get the idea.

So when I started worrying—and when I didn't want to do something because of my worry—Mom, of course, wanted **to make me feel better**. And believe me, I wasn't just politely letting her know I was worried. I would cry, beg, and tell her I was going to throw up—anything I could think of to get out of doing something I didn't want to do. I was such a mess that she wanted to do anything to make me comfortable again. That was her job, and she was terrific at it! And what she did worked. **Or so we thought**.

If I didn't want to ride a roller coaster, she wouldn't make me (not a big deal), and not riding made me feel better. When I started having trouble sleeping in my bed, she let me sleep in her room, and that *really* made me feel better. There were even some things that made *her* worry (like letting me ride the bus to school), so she wouldn't make me try them, which meant *both* of us felt better. And, really, who could blame us? If you have a fear or a worry, and you get away from the thing that makes you worry, then you feel better. Makes perfect sense, doesn't it?

Yeah, **if you want your worry to get bigger**, it makes perfect sense. That's what happened to me. As Mom and I allowed me to *avoid* all those different scary things, worry started to control more of my life.

Why? Because Mom and I made this our number one goal: to *avoid* anything that scared me. Mom helped me avoid because she wanted me to feel comfortable. She wanted me to stop freaking out. When she didn't push me, and let me avoid, I did stop freaking out. We gave in to worry because we didn't know what else to do. Worry got bigger, and my life got smaller. I didn't ride the bus; I stopped spending the night at friends' houses; I didn't even sleep alone in my own room anymore.

Parents help worry get stronger by helping kids AVOID things that scare them, by keeping them comfortable all the time. Or by trying. Elliot used to ask Mom over and over if he was safe at school. And she would constantly reassure him. "Of course you're safe at school. There are lots of adults to keep you safe." Elliot would feel better for a while, but the question kept coming back, and Mom kept saying what she needed to say to *keep him comfortable*. Looking for reassurance is just another way to avoid dealing with scary things, because Elliot never learned how to manage his fear. He just depended on Mom to keep it at a distance.

Keeping someone comfortable all the time is an impossible job, really, because being scared is a normal response. If a big dog comes charging at you, you're supposed to feel afraid. The first time you ride the school bus, you're going to worry. Feeling scared and worrying is going to happen, so you need to expect it and somehow get through it, not avoid it. It will get easier, I promise (because I'm going to give you some great tips to help). But if you keep going out of your way to avoid feeling worried or afraid, you don't get any practice feeling uncomfortable, and you don't learn how to get through it. You and your parents will have to let you feel uncomfortable. It's going to be different, for them and for you.

Is that hard to hear? I get it. If I invented some **magic potion to make worry disappear**, I'd be the richest girl in the country. Parents and kids would line up to buy it by the gallon. But there's no such potion, which means you're going to have to learn how to handle your feelings and to have a plan for dealing with your worry. Oh, a plan? You need a plan? How convenient we found each other then! Keep reading, please. Because if we're going to fix things, we need to know more about what we're up against.

What's Next?

Here's what we know so far: the genes we come with and the things our parents teach us can both influence how much we worry. In the next chapter, I'm going to tell you about more things that might make kids worry. Get ready to learn about turtles, airplanes, Marsh Man, and spaghetti. I'm serious. Spaghetti.

Chapter 3: Stop the World! I Want to Get Off

Every so often when I'm over at my friend's house, her older brothers play video games. The screen shows people getting killed or blown up. I know it's fake, but it's violent and gross. One day when I was there, the video game was blaring and the news was on the television. Then her dad came home late, and we had to rush to get my friend to her piano lesson. We got our shoes on quickly and dashed to the car.

When I finally walked into my house, Mom looked at me, cocked her head to the side, and asked, "What happened to you?" She could see that my eyes were big and **my shoulders were stuck in a permanent shrug**, up around my ears. Just being in the midst of all that loud rushing made my body feel wound up. There wasn't any *real* danger around me, but my body and my mind moved into fight-or-flight mode. I needed some quiet time to catch my breath and slow down.

I seem to get bothered by small things that don't bother other kids. A few months ago, I saw a movie with my friend. As usual, before it started, the trailers for other movies played. They were so loud, and images kept flashing on the screen, one after another. I put my hands over my ears and closed my eyes. **It was just too much**.

If you're like me, then you may notice how a lot of little things can add up and cause us problems, including the loud, scary, fast stuff. The stuff we wish we didn't know about, or see, and the stuff that keeps coming at us. This *is* a fast, loud world, and we can't help getting caught up in it sometimes. Every so often, I get this picture in my mind of us kids, standing with our bodies all stiff and tight, watching the world go whizzing by. We're like **turtles trying to cross a busy street**.

Grown-ups call this *stress*. They talk about it lots. At least around me they do. It comes from jobs and traffic and money. For kids, it comes from school and homework, family problems and friend problems. From trying to do too much or learn too much. From thinking we have to have it all figured out. It can make us feel like we're absorbing all the tensions of the world into our body, just as if we're sponges. That stress makes us anxious and worried.

Back when I was worrying a lot, I used to hear Mom say, "Casey, I just need more hours in the day. I'll never get it all done." We've both learned a lot since then, and now mom and I have worked on making our days slower and our tasks fewer. Now we think about how Mom's grandmother used to describe her perfect day: "Nowhere to go and all day to get there." Doesn't that sound better? Doesn't that *feel* better? It makes me **breathe slower and deeper** just thinking about it.

So, in summary… the stress of the outside world can make us anxious and worried, and there's not too much we kids can do about a lot of that outside world stuff. But learning how to manage what happens **inside of us** can definitely help us cope better with the stuff that happens on the outside. I've got a ton of cool things to teach you, so keep going!

Imagine That!

A few years ago, my cousin was telling me about the camping trip her family took to Grand Tetons National Park in Wyoming. One afternoon she was taking a hike by herself. It was really hot and sunny, and as she walked along, her mouth became drier and drier. She didn't have any more water in her daypack, and all she wanted was to satisfy her thirst. She started thinking about what she wanted to drink *right then*. Maybe a glass of lemonade. Or cold water with ice cubes. She could just taste it.

As she was telling me this story, I started having the same thirsty sensations. My mouth felt dry, and I needed a drink. I was parched! When she mentioned that lemonade, I was ready for a big gulp.

And if right now you start telling me about some fresh-baked chocolate chip cookies just coming out of the oven—those soft, warm chips of chocolate and that yummy buttery taste—my mouth will water. I'll even imagine **drinking a cold glass of milk between bites**.

If you describe to me the time you had seven mosquito bites on your ankles, I'll probably feel an itch or two, and maybe I'll have to scratch a bit.

Get the idea? Thinking about something—really imagining it—can make you *feel* something in your body. It's powerful. It's a big part of how we think and create and learn. And it can be really fun. Imagining is like building a bridge between your past and right now, or between today and your future. You can also rehearse something, try out a new idea, or practice a skill, all safely inside your mind. What do you think are of some of the coolest inventions we have in the world? I'll guess that each one started when someone imagined them. With thought and focus and work, they made these imagined ideas become real.

But we don't always imagine good things. We can powerfully rehearse bad things, too. Worry gets stronger when we keep **calling up scary stories** in our minds—ones that create scary sensations in our bodies. It's like reading a book and getting really absorbed in the story. But you're not reading a fun book; you're reading a book that makes you feel very uncomfortable.

Remember in the first chapter, I was writing about my encounter with the dog? There I was, sitting comfortably on my bed, writing to you, and I started feeling my heart race and my hands get clammy. That's an example of what I'm talking about—I was safe, but I felt scared again.

What if you're afraid to spend the night at a friend's house? When you think about going, you might imagine bad things happening, like having nightmares, or getting sick to your stomach. Maybe you picture waking your parents up in the middle of the night and making them come get you. As you imagine the possibility of all that bad stuff happening, you are rehearsing your fearful scenes in your mind, and your body starts reacting to what you picture. Your heart beats faster, and your stomach feels a little queasy. If I said to you, "Hey, want to spend the night at my house tonight?" and your mind immediately took you through all those terrible events, would you ever agree to spend the night? No way!

This is one way we **learn to avoid things**. Think of it as a series of steps. When we consider doing some activity (like spending the night out), and we picture that activity as unsafe, then we start feeling scared. So we worry about it. If we can't figure out how to feel safe, we avoid that activity. When we decide to avoid, we feel better, and we're *glad* we avoided. Then we'll want to avoid the next time, since that's the only thing we figured out that made us feel better this time. Here, let me draw you a chart.

How to be afraid of spending the night at a friend's house

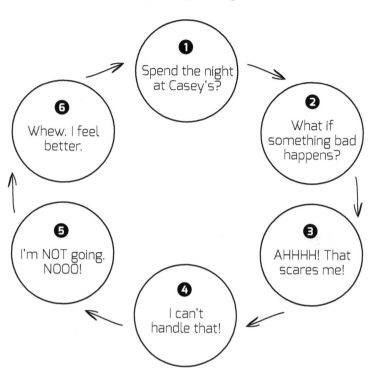

Getting really absorbed in your own thoughts and inviting your body along for the ride is a surefire way to make worry stronger. I was an expert at imagining danger. I could create bad endings to things that hadn't even happened yet! I needed a new plan to stop this pattern from ruining all my fun. Then, as I was learning about the power of imagination, I discovered something very cool. In Elliot's comic books.

You see, my brother Elliot loves comic books. The superhero kind. Adventures with bad guys and saving-the-world kind of stuff. He's getting much better at reading by himself, but sometimes I read aloud to him when he's tired of doing his own reading. A few months ago, right on page 17 of Marsh Man Battles the Swamp Lizard, I realized something important, so pay attention. Most of the superheroes in the comic books have some weird accident that gives them their superpowers. An experiment goes wrong in the chemistry lab, or some mutant snake bites them, and they find themselves with super strength, or vision, or taste buds, or something. Once they discover the power, they have to decide **what to do with this power**. Are they going to use it for good or for evil? Are they going to use it to rob the bank, or to catch the bank robbers? On page 17 of that comic book, I recognized you and me.

You and I have our own superpower called our imagination. It can make all sorts of things happen. It can build all sorts of bridges. It's rather fantastic. Perhaps, like me, you have stories of how your worry grew stronger after you imagined trouble. How it made you start backing away from an activity. Or maybe you started asking your parents questions like, "Am I okay? Is everything safe? Is there a monster under my bed?" (There's that reassurance thing I told you about.) Or maybe you had to do certain things to keep your imagination under control, like turn on all the lights in the house, or have your parents check under your bed 82 times before you fell asleep.

Would you like to create some different stories? Do you want to learn how your imagination could help? Hey, if Marsh Man can do it, you can, too. So you'll find that in our plan later on.

A Cooked Spaghetti Noodle

Imagine an *uncooked* spaghetti noodle, like when you first take it out of the box. Yes, I mean stop, close your eyes, and imagine it. I'll wait right here.

Got it? Now imagine trying to bend it in half without snapping it. Got it? What happened?

OK, now imagine a *cooked* spaghetti noodle, sitting on your plate, sauce or no sauce. That noodle can bend and squiggle, so make it into a circle, or a letter S. How about a bracelet? Or a pair of glasses? It's so flexible.

A lot of **worried kids are like the uncooked spaghetti**: rigid, stiff, and not flexible. One of the worry experts I met said that worry gets stronger when kids get *rigid*. What does he mean by that? He's saying that when kids need things to be very predictable, they will worry when things change. (That's being rigid.) If something is new or different (like a substitute teacher at school, or a broken nightlight), then a worried kid says something like, "Hey, this isn't what I planned! I didn't expect this at all. This is a surprise, and I can't handle it!" I can hear that spaghetti snap. Can you?

Worry also gets stronger when kids think they have to be perfect. Being perfect sounds pretty good, doesn't it? Who wouldn't want to be perfect? Imagine getting perfect grades on all your assignments! Riding your bike perfectly! Carrying a perfect tune! Perfect, though, quickly turns into another word for rigid. Worry grows when kids (or grown-ups) **believe there is only one perfect way** to get the job done and that mistakes are forbidden or terrible.

No mistakes? Do you remember learning how to walk? Me neither, but I watched Elliot learn. He fell all the time. On his fanny and on his face. Once, as he was losing his balance at a restaurant, he grabbed the tablecloth on the way to the floor, and pulled down two bowls of milk and cereal and a plastic glass of orange juice, too. (I didn't laugh… out loud, at least.) What if Mom had said to him, "Sorry, Elliot, but no mistakes here. Please don't walk again until you can do it perfectly"?

If you weren't allowed to make mistakes, would you have learned to ride a bike?

Eat with a fork?

Zip up your coat?

Write the alphabet?

When worry tells you to be perfect, it's **another way of saying STOP.** I remember in fourth grade I had to make a poster for my owl project. From the beginning, I just *knew* I wouldn't be able to make the owl look like the picture in my book. I knew it wouldn't be perfect, but I also knew I had to hand it in to the teacher. I kept putting it off. Night after night, I thought about the owl poster, but I couldn't bear to start drawing and make mistakes. I might as well have stuck a stop sign between that poster and me. The night before it was due, **I cried and cried**. I finally finished the poster, but only because I ran out of time and Mom made me go to bed. When I handed it in, I felt lousy. It wasn't perfect, and nothing short of perfect felt right to me. (Fourth grade was all-around hard for me. I'll tell you more about it in Chapter 9.)

I've been working on this "perfect" thing. I notice that when I can be a cooked spaghetti noodle—when I can accept what I'm able to do, even when it's not up to my "perfect" standards—then I'm not so stressed out. I discover that mistakes, when I do make them, aren't really as bad as I had imagined. So I'm more flexible now.

Sure, there are a few places where being perfect is necessary. If you worked in a chemistry lab, looking for the cure for a disease, you'd want to measure the chemicals perfectly during your experiment, so you could know what worked and what didn't. But fortunately, we've got a few years before we'll have to be that kind of perfect.

Being **flexible as cooked spaghetti** is definitely a part of my plan for you. You're going to experiment and make adjustments. You're going to screw up. In fact, you might even decide to make mistakes *on purpose*. Why? Because you'll discover that at first you'll feel uncomfortable and then you'll feel better. Handling discomfort is a lot easier when you know it'll only last a short while.

Taking the Stage

When I worried—which often meant I avoided things, refused to go places, and was sometimes just a stubborn pain in the neck about stuff—many times my mom gave in and let me stay home. But sometimes she got frustrated and forced me to do something I was refusing to do. She told me to "just deal with it." I went, but usually I cried or even yelled. By that point Mom usually got quiet, because explaining *again* why she needed me to cooperate did no good. I know (because she told me) that she tried not to cry, too, and she felt like a horrible parent.

Looking back, I see how my worries made our lives tricky. My mom needed to get to work or do the grocery shopping. Sometimes she just wanted to get some sleep. And I needed to go to school, learn new things, get my rest, and be a kid! She forced me to do stuff because sometimes it was the only strategy she could think of. But when she forced me, I ended up feeling panicked and lost.

I used to have this awful dream that someone pushed me out onto a stage in front of a huge audience. The music started, and I was supposed to sing, but I didn't know the song or the words. Everyone watching expected me to do something, but I couldn't. In the dream, I'd yell, "**How can I sing when I don't know the song?!**"

My dream was about being forced and feeling unprepared. My dream created those same uncomfortable feelings you might get when you think about having to *do* something about your worries. If you don't know what to do, or you don't think you have the tools for the job, you'll feel forced to do something you are not prepared for. And, of course, you'll feel scared.

My job is to prepare you, just like your baseball coach gives you batting practice before the game, or your music teacher has you sing the songs over and over again to get ready for the recital. When you actually start *doing something* about your worries, you're going to feel prepared. I promise you that. Not invincible, of course. Not even all that comfortable. But prepared. Maybe even excited? A girl can hope.

What's Next?

I've given you lots of information so far. You now know (in addition to all that stuff about genes and parents) that stress, your amazing imagination, and being too rigid also make worry stronger. Next I'm going to fascinate you with some facts about boredom, and surprise you with expectation. Wondering what I'm talking about? Good. Then move along. I'll meet you there.

Chapter 4: Great Expectations

In case anyone decides to give you a pop quiz on "Why do we worry?" here are the answers we've come up with. We kids worry because…

- Worry helps us slow down when it's smart to take our time, back away from things when it's smart to avoid, and run away or fight when the danger is real.
- Plus, some of us might be more likely to worry because of our biological make-up (our genes).
- And, some parents unknowingly teach us to worry by the ways they act.
- The world can be a fast and stressful place, and sometimes we take on too much.
- Also, with our creative minds, we can imagine all kinds of problems that scare us!
- In addition, some of us want everything to always work out perfectly. We get as rigid as a dry noodle. If we're not sure how things will turn out, then we worry.

Are you ready if there's a pop quiz? Here's a shortcut version of these five reasons why kids worry:

- It can sometimes help us

- Our genes
- Learning from our parents
- The stress of the world
- Our imaginations!
- Being rigid as a dry noodle

One day, as I was studying all of this, suddenly a message popped into my mind, like a voice from my internal coach. "EXPECT TO WORRY." I knew just what it meant, and it became the first piece of the worry puzzle that Mom and I solved.

I used to wish I would never worry again. I thought "normal" kids went through their days feeling calm and relaxed about everything, and I wanted to be like them. On the first day of school, I actually believed that the other kids were completely comfortable with their new teachers, new classrooms, and new routines. I thought I needed to get rid of my worried thoughts completely, but that seemed impossible. Why did it seem impossible? Because it was... and IS!

It's normal to feel fear, and it's normal to have worried thoughts. I've stated it repeatedly now, haven't I? If you are alive, then you will feel fear, and your body will react. If you have a brain, you'll have tons of thoughts, and some of them will be worried thoughts. We're not going to get rid of them, so we better learn to manage them… to handle them differently.

And the first thing you need to do? **Stop being surprised** when your worries pop up. *Expect* those worried thoughts. Yep, they're coming. Take me, for instance. My worried thoughts don't surprise me anymore, especially when I'm learning something new or if I'm uncertain about how I'm going to handle something.

Oh, Hello, Worry! You Again?

Last summer, one of the girls on my soccer team invited me to a great birthday party at a water park, but the weather forecast called for a chance of thunderstorms in the afternoon. I was worried about that. I didn't want them to cancel the party, and I didn't want to get caught in a thunderstorm, either. When we arrived at the water park, I saw some dark clouds in the distance. I didn't know exactly how our day was going to turn out, so I worried a bit about stuff like this:

"What if it starts to thunder?"

"What if we don't get to swim?"

"Will they let us back in after the storm passes?"

"What if it pours, and all our stuff gets wet?"

If I had been in this situation a few years ago— before I knew how to handle my worried thoughts—I would have asked myself those same "what if" questions, and pretty quickly the inside of my head would have sounded something like this:

"I wonder if it'll be a bad storm. I don't want it to storm. I don't know what we'll do. Why does this have to happen? Wait, now I'm worrying! Why am I thinking this way again? I hate when I do this. People will notice me. I have to get out of here. I can't do this. I have to make it stop now. I need to feel better. Why is my heart pounding like this? I'm starting to feel hot. Am I sick? What if I faint? Or throw up? I can't handle this. There's something wrong with me, and I can't make it stop! I don't know what to do. I'm not normal."

When I look back on those years of worrying, I see now how familiar I was with my worried thoughts… painfully familiar. Still, they consistently seemed to catch me off guard. And they predictably ended with the announcement: "**And you, Casey, can't handle this!**"

If someone sings Happy Birthday to you *on your actual birthday*, are you surprised? No. If you walk outside on a sunny summer day and you feel warm, are you surprised? Of course not. But somehow I acted as if those worried thoughts of mine were breaking news.

I'm so much better than I was. Honestly, worries still pop up to bother me, but I can really, truly say I'm better. I'm better because I've changed how I respond to them. Now I expect to worry. I mean it. I know it's going to show up eventually, because it thinks it's taking care of me, keeping me safe. That afternoon at the water park, when I saw the clouds and heard the forecast, I imagined it spoiling our fun. Lots of kids had similar reactions. I recognized that I was worrying, and this is how I greeted my worried thoughts:

"Oh, hi, worry. It's you again. Yeah, I was thinking you might show up. I don't know what's going to happen with this thunderstorm today, so some what-if-ing is to be expected. I'm not surprised to hear from you. Some worry is normal."

(By the way—yes, I talk to my worry. And I'm not crazy. In the next chapter, I'm going to teach you how to do it, too. Very helpful!)

Do you know one of the reasons I had fun at the water park that day? *I expected worry to show up.* The thunderstorm never got close to us, by the way, so I'm glad my worry didn't ruin the whole party for me. Most of my friends had the same what-if questions. We all wanted some information, but we just had to wait and see what the storm did.

So, the first way to handle worry is: EXPECT IT.

If you don't let it surprise you, then your first response to your worry can be different. Let me give you a non-worry example. Last week I made plans for my friend Jess to come over at 2:00. When the doorbell rang at 2:02, I opened the front door. There stood Jess. I said hello and let her in. Simple.

Now, imagine instead that I called Jess to come over, and Jess said, "I'd love to, Casey. But I've already made plans to visit my cousins all afternoon." Then, at 2:30, the doorbell rings, and when I open the door, Jess is standing there. I'd have a very different reaction, wouldn't I? I'd say "Hello!" But my eyes might be open wide, with my eyebrows up, and I'd ask her a bunch of questions. Surprise just feels and sounds different.

Okay, how about this? What if I make plans for Jess to come over at 2:00, the doorbell rings at 2:02, and when I open the door, there stands Jess…and yet I'm surprised, with those confused questions and those wide open eyes? Does that make sense? Hardly. But I'll bet that's how you react when worry shows up. Worry comes pretty often in a kid's life. Yet every time it shows up, we tend to get surprised by it. Even alarmed. "Oh, no! I'm worried about getting called on in class tomorrow! This is terrible! I should get *more* worried about the fact that I'm worried. And now my stomach aches. This means tomorrow is going to be awful! I better worry more!"

Surprise happens, of course, and sometimes it's fun. But my mom and I realized that if I can get over being surprised when worry pops up, I'll feel more in charge almost immediately. We had figured out *why* I worried (genes and being rigid and all that stuff we've already talked about). Now we wanted to know *when* I worried. If I can have a good guess about the times when I worry, then I won't be so surprised and I can also start planning *how* I want to respond. You see, understanding is a step-by-step process: figuring out why I worry, then when I worry, then how I want to respond when I worry.

It took us about four months to answer that question of when I worry. (It won't take you that long, because I'm going to help.) I started keeping a log of lots of the big and little times I worried. I had things on the list like, "I really want Jess to spend the night, and I'm afraid her mom's going to say no." Or, "I want to jump off the diving board, but I'm not sure I can hold my breath long enough to get up from the bottom of the deep end. And that diving board looks high!" Then I recruited Elliot to keep a list, too. I had to **bribe him** with **two packs of chewing gum** and taking over his emptying-the-dishwasher chore twice. Plus, he wouldn't write stuff down, so I had to keep interviewing him. "What kind of things scare you?" And, "did anything bother you today?" His list included "starting karate lessons" and "a dog chased after Boo this morning!"

After a while, I started to think that between us we worried about everything! But one night I marked all the items on our lists that sounded similar, and different clusters started to show up. Two categories jumped right out at me: when I'm doing something new or different, and when I'm unsure of my plans. Elliot had a similar set of worries. Then I found a big category for both of us: when we are about to perform. Then it all fell into place, and I found two more categories of worried times: when we have a lot of "what if" questions and when something scary is happening.

Casey's List of When to Expect Worry

- **I'm doing something new or different**: First day of school; Substitute teacher; Jumping off diving board
- **I have a lot of "what if" questions**: What if I get sick on our trip to the beach? What if I forget my homework? What if my

dog dies?

- **Worrying about performing**: Getting called on in Spanish; Running in cross-country meet
- **I'm unsure about my plans**: Jess needs to ask her mom if she could sleep over; It might rain the day we want to play miniature golf; Ice cream truck might run out of my favorite flavor
- **Something scary is happening**: Thunderstorm knocks out power in house; I have to get my tonsils out; Driving in a snowstorm & the road is slippery

Elliot's List of When to Expect Worry

- **I'm doing something new or different**: A new bus driver on the first day of school; Mom takes me to karate lessons; I'm flying on an airplane for first time
- **I have a lot of "what if" questions**: What if the movie previews are scary & loud? What if I need to go to the bathroom while I'm on the school bus? What if there's nothing I like to eat at the restaurant?
- **Worrying about performing**: Have to recite poem in class; Sparring in Karate
- **I'm unsure about my plans**: Go to the beach if Mom gets out of work early; David is not sure if he wants to sleep over my house, but I want him to!; Mom is thinking about changing jobs, so her schedule might be different
- **Something scary is happening**: Neighbor's dog is chasing our cat; I climb too high in tree at park; Casey is watching a scary show & I can hear it from my bed

Check these five categories out. Do they make sense to you? Kids and grownups can expect worry to arrive when:

- We're doing something new or different (especially if we need it to go exactly right)
- We're unsure about our plans (especially if we need to be sure)
- We have a lot of "what if" questions (especially if we need to answer all of them)
- We have to perform (especially if we don't feel prepared or we think we'll be criticized)
- Something scary or dangerous is happening

You know what's interesting? Most of the items on my list were not on Elliot's list *at all*! He loves thunderstorms, so if the power goes out, he's excited to get out the flashlights and the candles. And he likes about ten different flavors carried on the ice cream truck, so he never even thinks about that worry. I love flying on planes, so that only bothers me for a moment. I think we both have some worry on the first day of school, but I've discovered that almost all kids do. **Totally, perfectly normal**.

So... let's review what you should be learning. Can you guess what I'm going to say?

First, *expect to worry*, because...
- It's normal and can be helpful. Sometimes stopping and even backing away are smart moves.
- Plus, our parents, our genes, our *great* imaginations, and wanting everything to go perfectly—all these contribute to more worries.

And, second, *expect to worry*, because it shows up whenever...
- you're doing something new or different
- you're unsure about your plans
- you have a lot of "what if" questions

- you have to perform
- something scary is happening

If these two points make sense to you—the why's and the when's of worry—then you're moving from just being familiar with worry to understanding worry. And this brings us to a whole new set of questions:

- Why does worry show up when we're doing something new or different?
- What makes us worry when we're not sure of our plans?
- When we have to perform, what is the purpose of all that worry?
- What's the benefit of worries that come as a bunch of "what if's"?
- What good is worry when something scary starts happening?

Here's the answer to all those questions (drum roll, please). It *thinks* it's helping you! Worry is saying, "There could be a problem here! And if there is, you have to fix it!"

There's nothing wrong with suddenly having worries. If a kid never worries then he or she is **probably living a pretty boring life**. Each new and different thing that we do as we grow up will involve doubt. "Can I do this? Will I like it? What will happen?" When it's new and different, we don't know how it will turn out, and it might not go according to plan. Or we don't *have* a plan. So worry says, "Uh, oh. Better get ready." Worries can be good signals that we're exploring new territory.

Here's the thing…

Worry is SOMETIMES helpful, because it gets us to slow down or back away when we need time to figure out what to do (like reminding you to put on your bike helmet).

And sometimes it isn't (like worrying that your feet might one day outgrow your favorite shoes).

But...**worry ALWAYS thinks it's being helpful**, even when it's not.

So... our job is to decide when to listen to our worries and when to *ignore* them. We CANNOT allow our worries to run the show. If we let our worries control our decisions, we'll *keep* slowing down and backing away, and our lives will get really small and boring.

If worry is running *your* show, I predict that you have three troubles (because I had these same ones). First, you keep worrying and worrying instead of figuring out how to fix the problem. Second, worrying over and over can make small problems start to feel like REALLY BIG PROBLEMS. When you think that you are facing REALLY BIG PROBLEMS, you tend to back away from them. At least that's what I did.

And, third, your worries don't always come in little doses, either. They're not the "sometimes" and "helpful" variety, but have become more like the too-much-of-the-time and not-at-all-helpful type. I think my friend Jane (she's a grownup) says it well. She describes her worry as being like salt, sun, and ice cream. "Casey," she says, "I like salt on my French fries, sun on my face, and ice cream in my tummy. But too much of any of those makes me pretty uncomfortable."

What's Next

You understand so much more about worrying, don't you? No more treating your worried thoughts like breaking news (because you know to expect them.) No more being surprised by thoughts that aren't very surprising (because you've had them before.) You understand that worry—like heat in the summer, or the moon shining at night—is going to make an appearance. You know how bossy and controlling worry can be, and how it can make your life duller and your world smaller.

Next, we're going to look at ways to solve some of those problems before you get all upset by the too-much and not-helpful worries. We'll talk about ways to bring those REALLY BIG PROBLEMS and your too-big worries back down to a manageable size. All that's coming up.

Chapter 5: Chatting with the Squirrel

When I was in fifth grade, there was a kid named Trevor who consistently cut in front of us in the lunch line. He'd walk up, whistle or hum, then slip in front of some little first grader. We all knew he was going to do it. We expected it. He'd cut in, keep whistling, and shuffle a bit while looking at his shoes. And we'd yell, "Treee-vooor, back to the end of the line!" It wasn't enough to just expect he was going to cut. We couldn't just *know* that he was up to something. We had to <u>act</u>. We had to send him back to where he belonged and stick up for the little first grader, right?

That's what you and I are going to do with worry. To *expect* that you will worry is only the start. Once the worry is here, you need to learn what to do with it. It's time to put worry back where it belongs. Remember, worry thinks it's taking care of you, so it's going to keep intruding into your thoughts about trying new activities. You might say it's gotten **too big and bossy**, always stepping in and taking charge. And when worry is in charge, it has an enormous impact on you and your family. Go ahead and ask your family members. I'll wait.

Sometimes I hear parents say, "Oh, my son is just a worrier! That's who he *is*." At one point, I think my mom would have described me that way, too. It did seem like worrying was my full-time job, because it took up a lot of our week. All that stopping and avoiding and refusing and panicking. I know now that worrying is not *all* that I am, but it is a *part* of me that I can manage.

Worrying is not all of you, either, but right now it might feel like an awfully big part of you. When people call you a worrier, it's usually because they see the worrying part taking charge of too many of your decisions. They begin to believe—and you do, too—that the strength and size of your worry is as permanent as your eye color or that birthmark behind your left knee.

Believe me, I get it. When I was younger, my worry (as I've told you a gazillion times now) was way too big and unbelievably bossy. I had no a clue what to do. If my worry was Trevor, I was letting him cut in the lunch line while I acted surprised. And I wouldn't do anything about it.

Until… I met this girl in the waiting room at the doctor's office (not my favorite place, by the way.)

A Mouse—On My Shoulder

I was almost ten and just beginning to learn about managing worry. (It wasn't long after I'd puked on my green dress, actually.) I was sitting in the waiting room at our doctor's office while Mom was in with Elliot. I was alone except for another girl sitting across from me. We were about the same size. She was swinging her feet. After a few minutes, I called out to her (I may have been a worrier but I've never been shy, remember), "I hate coming here. I have to get a shot. It makes me feel bad."

"I don't like shots either," she said back. "I have to get one, too. My worry is all freaked out, but **I'm talkin' her down.**"

"What? Her worry is all freaked out?" That's what I asked in my head. "What? Your worry is all freaked out?" That's what I asked out loud.

"Sure," she responded. "We all have worry. Mine always shows up at the doctor's office, so now I just expect her. I can't blame her, 'cause shots hurt. But I get through it. I used to lose it! My worry would tell me to run for my life. I'd cry and feel sick to my stomach. It was terrible."

This was sounding a little familiar (okay, more than a little). I put my chin in my hands, my elbows on my knees, and leaned forward. "And...?" I asked.

"Now I imagine my worry as a mouse. On my shoulder. Yelling in my ear. Always says the same stuff. Tells me how much shots hurt, how gross they are. I hear it, but I'm not surprised by it. It's not breaking news. I do feel sort of nervous right now. I feel a little cold, and I'm sure my heart is beating kinda fast. But I can handle it. That mouse just talks, and I just hear it. Who likes getting a shot, anyway? But I've done it before. I'm going to feel nervous, and then it's going to be over. That's what I say to myself, and to my worry."

This was surprising news to me. I didn't have to believe my worried thoughts? I could hear them, and I could even *feel uncomfortable* in my body, and still not put worry in charge? I talked to this girl for a few more minutes, until we both went in for our shots. Right then and there I started practicing her techniques. I was nervous and shaky, but I sat through that shot, with worry talking up a storm in my ear! Every time I heard the worried thoughts, I reassured myself, "That's my normal worry talking." And I got through it. I did something differently. I reacted differently. It was a great start. It wasn't fun, and—to be honest—it wasn't even easy. But I didn't scream or panic or run away. I'd describe it as *easier*.

"Hey! This is another piece to the puzzle!" That's what I said to myself last year as I was figuring all this stuff out. And now I say it to you. This is another piece to the puzzle! "TALK TO YOUR WORRY."

Chatting with the Squirrel

What did I do? First, I *externalized* my worry, although I didn't know it at the time. That's a word I learned from the experts, and it means that I put my worried voice outside of myself, by using my imagination.

The girl I met in the doctor's office externalized her worry by making it a mouse sitting on her shoulder. I think that day I **borrowed her mouse, too**! But soon, I gave my worry the identity of a *squirrel*. Are you familiar with squirrels? Especially squirrels who are irritating? Or annoying? Or trying to get your attention? They chatter. And chatter. And because they do their chattering from the safety of a very tall branch, it's quite impossible to shut them up. It seems rather fitting. My worry—my chattering squirrel—has a tendency to keep up the noise longer than I'd like. What's changed? Now I don't have to listen.

My imagination has changed my worry identity over the years. Sometimes it's that same chattering squirrel, and other times it's a stubborn version of me, that rigid piece of uncooked spaghetti. I talked to one kid who made his worry a big piece of talking bubble gum.

You get to choose how you **imagine your worried voice**. It doesn't matter what it looks like or sounds like, as long as you imagine it *outside* of yourself. Separate yourself from those powerful thoughts and feelings for a few moments; give yourself a little distance from the worry. It's like taking a few steps back from a huge, wall-size painting in a museum so you can see it better, or taking a break from a science project for school so you can clear your head.

My mom recently learned this little trick to keep her from getting too busy and stressed: when someone asks her to do something (like volunteer on a school committee or babysit for her friend's kids), she can hear a little voice in her mind saying, "I should say 'yes.' They need my help." Then she steps back and gets a little distance from that voice before she makes her decision. She doesn't want to react too quickly and get sucked into too many commitments. To the other person she then says, "Let me think about it and check my schedule. I'll get back to you on that." My mom, the Externalizer.

I'd never heard her using this I'll-get-back-to-you answer before, so when I noticed her talking that way, I paid attention. Being the student of handling worry that I am, I wondered how I might use that approach. Could I talk to my worry like my mom talked to the head of the school volunteers? What a curious idea…and it didn't take long for an opportunity to arise. It gave me a chance to put my worry outside of me and talk directly to it, without getting sucked in.

This is how it happened: a few weeks later I was studying for a math test, and my worry showed up. Some of the practice questions were tough, and I felt my frustration growing. Taking tests makes me nervous anyway (I think most kids feel that way), so the muscles in my neck tightened. My heart was beating fast. I could feel the tears welling up. I wanted to throw my pencil or break it in half.

Somewhere in the middle of all that, I noticed my worry chattering up a storm (which did not surprise me, by the way.) "Do you *really* think you can learn this? What if you don't have enough time? What if you fail? Is this going to be on the test? What is your *problem*?"

I put down my pencil (instead of throwing it), sat back in my chair, and said out loud, "Hmmm, worry, let me take a break, and I'll get back to you on that." I stood up, went to the kitchen, ate fourteen chocolate covered raisins and petted the cat. I imagined my worry as a chattering squirrel, wringing its little paws, and I said to it (this time in my head because Elliot was in the kitchen with his friend), "**Worry, I can learn this math stuff**. I need to review. That's why I'm studying. I've got plenty of time. And you're not helping, by the way. I'm going to ignore you now."

My muscles relaxed a bit, and I felt *less* like crying. I still wasn't excited about studying for my math test, but I consider that a fairly normal reaction. I headed back to my math book, finished up one of those tough problems, and then kept plodding forward. Fun? Not at all. Manageable? Definitely.

As I continued to study, my worry hung around, being quiet sometimes and noisy at other times. I must have talked to my worry about six or seven more times just during that one afternoon. With practice, it became easier. And our conversations became shorter. Worry would say, "Uh-oh, this is a hard problem. What if you can't...." Then I would interrupt the worried thought. Just stop it in its tracks. "We don't need to repeat this again," I'd say. Or, "**I know you're there, but I'm busy**."

As time passed, my mind and body became calmer, quieter. Looser muscles, no tears, and not a single thrown pencil. I did sigh a lot, and put my forehead down on the table a few times. When I noticed my thoughts and feelings moving more toward *panicky* (tight muscles, the start of tears), I got up and took a break for a few minutes. (And, yes, I finished off the chocolate-covered raisins.) Then I talked to my worry again. At one point I even became so annoyed with that irritating squirrel chatter that I told my worry to KNOCK IT OFF!

Which brings me to an important announcement you need to hear before we go a page farther.

Big Announcement! There Are Different Ways of Talking to Worry

"That's it?" you say. "That's the big announcement?" Yes, that's it: different kids talk to their worry in different ways. Some kids change up how they talk to it, depending on the situation. You get to choose how you talk to your worry.

As I was putting this book together for you, I talked to a lot of kids. I wanted to know how other kids managed their worries. Often their ideas or strategies were similar to what I used, but with a different little twist or approach. (That's how I found out about the talking bubblegum, by the way.)

I guess it's like my Aunt Lisa's recipes for chili or apple pie or brownies... a little more of this, or a touch of that, or a secret ingredient that adds a different flavor altogether. My Aunt Lisa is an amazing cook, and it's mainly because she can take a recipe from somewhere and adapt it to what she or her guests like. Can't eat meat? She'll make a meatless chili for you. Love walnuts? She'll add them to the brownies. She has a recipe for chocolate cake that uses vinegar. Yes, vinegar. It's crazy delicious.

When it comes to talking to worry—how we react to it and what we say to it—kids are creative and adaptable, like Aunt Lisa. Some kids are kind to their worries, and others are far less sympathetic. When I was studying for my math test, I stepped back from my worry and talked to it calmly at times. But my worry also irritated me, so I was a bit blunt with it, too. More of that noodle flexibility, right there.

Some kids even **invite the worry along** on their adventure because it helps them stay safe. If you're skateboarding home from school, worry can remind you to watch out for those big cracks in the sidewalk in front of the Cooks' house.

"I Know You're Just Trying to Do Your Job"

My friend Kate told me about her bedtime worry. When it began a few years ago, it came at her fast and furious, just as soon as her parents turned off her light and left her bedroom. Her worry told her that someone was in the closet, and even after she turned on her light and checked the closet over and over, the worried thoughts still said the same thing. She worried that someone was going to come into the house and take her or kill her family. She heard of such things happening on the news. Her house was in a safe neighborhood, and it even had an alarm system, but those facts didn't matter. Every night those worried thoughts arrived at bedtime, saying the same things.

Soon, Kate began anticipating the worry long before bedtime. She imagined vividly how awful it made her feel, so that by the end of dinner her stomach was in knots and her body trembled. She couldn't even eat sometimes. Her parents were stumped. Nothing seemed to help. After hearing her check the closet and walk out into the hall over and over, one of her parents would give in and come sit with her. Eventually, Kate could only fall asleep if her mom or dad were sitting on her bed.

Kate's parents arranged for her to meet with Mrs. Ellsbury, the counselor at school, hoping Mrs. Ellsbury knew how to handle worry. The counselor told Kate some of the very things I learned: worried thoughts usually say the same things over and over again, so treating them like a surprise, night after night, only made her more frightened and the thoughts more powerful. Mrs. Ellsbury told Kate she'd have to let the worried thoughts know she was onto them, and figure out how to take charge.

They did some planning and practicing together, and Kate came up with her approach. When the worried thoughts showed up at dinner, Kate was ready to say, "Look, I'm sick of you here! **Go away and leave me alone!**" Curiously, though, when they did arrive, Kate's plan didn't seem to fit.

You see, when Kate decided to externalize her worry, she imagined it as a scared rabbit, with **big brown eyes and a nervously twitching nose**. She saw the rabbit as trying to warn and protect her. She didn't want to be mean and bossy. It didn't feel right to her. So she said this instead: "I know you're just trying to do your job. And if I'm really in danger, you will alert me, I'm sure. But you are convincing me to be scared in a very safe house. You're telling me someone is hiding in the closet, even after I've checked carefully. I'll expect you at bedtime, but when you show up, I'll tell you we're both going to be fine. I can handle going to bed."

When Kate told the counselor her strategy for talking to her worried thoughts, the counselor was impressed. "You're expecting the worried thoughts to show up, and you're learning to handle them. You're allowing them to be there, and you're doing okay. That's wonderful, Kate." (School counselors love to use the word "wonderful.")

Kate realized how intently she had been listening to her worried thoughts and how repetitive they were. So she shifted her reaction to them. For several nights, Kate still felt worried at bedtime. When she turned off her lights, the worry rabbit part absolutely wanted to check the closet and call her parents. What helped her get through those worried moments? She didn't let herself be surprised by the thoughts anymore. She stepped back and talked to the worry. After about a week of practice, she was able to give worry an even briefer message: "I'm safe. I'm going to sleep now." She told me how she sometimes imagines **tucking that worried rabbit into bed** with her, and keeping *it* safe for the night!

Knocking a Fly Out of the Park

When my brother Elliot started having some worry trouble at baseball practice, I told him about Kate. "So why don't you imagine those worries as little rabbits, like Kate did? Tell them it's okay if they come to baseball practice. Tell them you understand." He looked at me with a scowl. "Are you nuts?" he said, and walked away, dragging his bat behind him.

Here's what he did instead to manage those baseball worries.

Elliot has loved baseball for as long as I can remember. He started when he was six, hitting off a big tee. No strike outs or walks. No pitches. Then he moved up to coach pitch. The coaches lobbed the ball in gently, so that the kids could learn to swing and hit. No problem.

Last spring, he moved up to kid pitch. Strikes and balls and outs and other kids pitching the ball at him. Kids that weren't so great at pitching, by the way. It was a change.

After a few practices, Elliot announced to Mom that he was quitting baseball. "But you love baseball," Mom said. "What happened?" After several "nothing's" (my mom wasn't buying that), Elliot confessed he was worried about getting hit by a pitch. He'd already seen professional ball players get hit on TV, and two kids on his team had been hit. It hurts. He might bleed. He was so worried about getting hit that he was backing up every time a pitch came near him, and he wasn't swinging or hitting at all.

(This is when I suggested he imagine his worries were Kate-like rabbits. **He asked me if I was nuts** and then walked away. Now you're all caught up.)

Our mom—who was fast becoming a worry-managing all-star— followed Elliot up to his room. (I followed her, and listened from the hall. Please, I'm just curious. And it's helping you, isn't it?) Elliot had his arms crossed, and his face was scrunched up. He angrily stomped his feet a few times. When he spoke next, his arms were down by his side, his elbows locked and his hands squeezed into fists. His face was red, and it wasn't because he was embarrassed. "I *love* playing baseball. The worry is ruining all my fun!" Elliot is also pretty competitive, and he knew the worry was making him a lousy hitter. Bottom line: he wanted to hit, win, and have fun, and his worry was in the way. Since he couldn't figure out what to do, he decided to quit.

Mom helped him describe this worry part, and Elliot imagined it as a **giant fly buzzing around** his head when he was up at the plate. "What if the ball hits you? It's going to hurt! What if you get a bloody nose? Stay out of the way. Ooooh, you're gonna strike out!"

Did he love baseball enough to get some bumps and bruises? Yes. And because the answer was yes, he needed to take a tough stance against the worry. "I'm not going to like getting hit with the ball, but *I can handle it*, and I need to focus on other things when I'm playing."

Elliot thought about what he wanted to say back to his worry. "Hey, you're ruining my fun, and I've had it with you. If I do pay attention to you, I just might get hit with the pitch! I'm gonna focus on hitting the ball. Maybe I'll pretend that the ball is a worry fly, and I'm going to smack it over the fence."

Elliot had no trouble being tough with this worry. It was annoying him, and he'd had it (like he said). If he stepped back from his worry, he could focus on hitting again. He understood that there were some things about baseball he didn't like much, but he could handle them. He might get hit with a baseball. If he did, it could possibly hurt. Or give him a bloody nose. Once, a kid on the team was hit and needed an ice pack for a few minutes. But then he was fine. Most of the time, when the pitch came in too close, kids were able to get out of the way.

Kate and Elliot had very different styles of talking to their worry. **The flexibility of cooked spaghetti**. It's a wonderful thing! And even though their *styles* were different, they both used the same tips you've been learning from me.

Let's review what we know so far about changing our reactions to worry. First, learn to accept that you will worry. In fact, *expect* worry. It's normal, and everyone has worried thoughts. That's what we talked about last chapter. Now I'm telling you to learn how to *talk* to your worry, and show your worry you can handle it. It's not the boss.

Kate talked to her worry gently. She gave her worry *permission* to show up, she understood it, and she handled it. I said the same kind of thing at the water park in the last chapter. "Oh, hi, worry. It's you again. I was thinking you might show up." Elliot talked *tough* to his worry. He wanted it gone, and he wasn't going to listen to it anymore. Both styles worked.

Different Ways Kids Can Talk to Worry

EXPECT IT	TAKE CARE OF IT	BOSS IT AROUND
I know you're just trying to help.	I'm going to feel nervous, and then it'll be over.	I'll get back to you on that, worry.
You usually show up at these times, so I'm not surprised by you.	It's OK; things will work out.	You're not helping. I'm going to ignore you.
Worry is a part of learning something new. I'm supposed to feel this way.	It's OK. I can handle whatever happens.	I know you're there, but I'm busy.
	I'm safe, even though I feel scared.	Knock it off! Stop trying to scare me!
		You're ruining my fun. I've <u>had</u> it with you.

Oh, yeah, really important point here. I'm not coaching you about how to talk to your worry so that it disappears. Sorry, not going to happen. Like we've talked about before, everybody's worries come and go. And come back again a few moments later. Remember: expect to worry. There is no way you can *banish* or *eliminate* your worries. And you don't need to banish them; you need to handle them.

What's Next?

Okay. We're really moving along now. Next step: I'm going to teach you how to handle your worries by being uncomfortable in a whole new way. You think you already know all about being uncomfortable, don't you? Think you're a regular expert at feeling uncomfortable, right? Well, there's a lot you *don't* know. Really. Let me explain...Oh, wait. This chapter is long enough already. Turn the page, and I'll enlighten you in the next chapter.

Chapter 6: Becoming Unglued

Alright…so…are you starting to get the idea that it's *possible* to listen in to your worried thoughts? And that you can talk to that worried voice inside you? Are you beginning to understand that you might have a few options about *how* you can talk to it?

I hope you can experiment with one or two of these ways to respond to your worried thoughts. You'll discover that there are times that you can gently set your worry aside. Or, if necessary, you can even elbow worry out of the way. When you handle your worries, you then have a chance to take charge. That'll make it easier for you to try new things, because you won't be scaring yourself so much.

As you learn—over time and with practice—to talk to your worries, and even challenge them (rather than just listening to them like they're breaking news), then you'll find your worries start quieting down. When worries quiet down, you then begin to talk to yourself with your <u>own</u> voice, the one you choose to have in those moments. You'll start talking to yourself about what you want to do. And talking to yourself in a very interesting way.

Have you ever seen how one adult welcomes another adult into a room, in kind of a formal way? Like for a job interview? It sounds something like this: "Hello, nice to meet you. Please come in and make yourself comfortable."

What if you came to see me for a job interview, and I said to you as I shook your hand: "Hello, how are you? Please, come in and allow yourself to be **uncomfortable. And uncertain, too**, while you're at it."

You'd probably think I was strange. Bizarre, even. Get uncomfortable? Be uncertain? Who would even suggest such a thing?

Me, that's who. And I have a very good reason for recommending such a thing. Two very good reasons, actually.

1. Being uncomfortable and uncertain is the price you pay for moving into new territory, and in order to grow you need to move into new territory. (Worry says STOP. Worry is not a big fan of moving forward.)
2. Being uncomfortable and uncertain, and handling it, resets your alarm system, and allows you to do what you want to do. (Worry fires off your alarm system, usually way too much.)

I fully accept that I have some convincing to do here. In fact, before I dove into this chapter, I made sure I was well rested and fully hydrated. I have some snacks right here, too. Just in case.

This is important stuff, and I'm ready.

First, I'm going to explain to you why it's so important that you get uncomfortable and uncertain. And why, to manage new and scary things, you should even be WILLING to feel that way. I'll do that in this chapter. Then, I have to show you how to reset your alarm system. How to talk to yourself in a new voice. How to step into **a big pile of uncertain discomfort**, and **walk out victorious**. On purpose. (That's in the next chapter.)

Believe me, I know how this sounds to you. But I also know how you think and how your worry operates, because I used to be right there with you.

So let's get to work on this, shall we? First up… being willing to be uncomfortable, because that's how you grow.

What DOESN'T Work

Remember, we've already established that worry exists to protect you. It only has two ways to measure whether you're safe.

- Are you feeling comfortable?
- Do you know for sure how everything is going to turn out?

If you're worrying, you're questioning if things are going to turn out the way you want them to. That's going to make you nervous, like you're shaking inside. When you get anxious like that, you think, "I've *gotta* get comfortable! Now!" And when you aren't sure whether some activity will turn out in your favor, you think, "I've *gotta* know that everything will go just right."

WRONG! I totally get why you think that way. But, nonetheless, it WON'T WORK! I've been there and done that for far too long. I *know* it doesn't work, because when you tell yourself that you need to be sure of how everything's going to turn out, and you always need to feel comfortable, then you won't be able to explore new activities.

This creates a pretty big problem, because whether you realize it right now or not, *your job, as a kid, is to grow.* And I don't mean just physically. You've got to grow in your skills, in your interests, in your smarts. We all do; that's how we grow *up*. How do you keep growing? By experimenting with new things, over and over again, for years. We've all been doing it since we were babies. I watched Elliot take his first steps. He stood. Wobbled. Fell. Stood, wobbled, fell. Stood, fell. Took a step. Now, seven years later, he plays baseball.

How might you feel when you experiment with new things? Uncomfortable, doubtful, awkward, embarrassed, clumsy, worried. It comes with the territory. You don't want to feel awkward? Don't want to feel *any* of those things? Then you'll get taller, but you won't grow.

The Blind Leading the Blind

You can bet that Spencer Silver and Arthur Fry know the benefits of not knowing how things are going to turn out but sticking with it anyway. Way back in 1970, in the 3M Corporation lab, Silver was researching ways to make stronger glue. Despite all his efforts, his invention wasn't good enough. Instead of creating a powerful adhesive, his bond was weaker that the traditional glue. He had no idea what to do with his result, but for the next five years, he continued to talk about it informally and in seminars with his colleagues.

Arthur Fry was one of those colleagues. Before he became a 3M scientist, he was a tinkerer throughout his childhood, always trying to figure things out. As a boy, he even engineered **custom-designed toboggans from scrap lumber**. And he sat in on one of Silver's meetings about the not-too-sticky adhesive. Fry also happened to sing in the church choir, and he had a minor little problem. Whenever he placed pieces of paper as page markers in the hymn book, some of them would fall out, and he'd lose his place. Sitting in on that meeting, Fry had an idea. "What if I put some of Spencer's glue on my page markers? Maybe that'll hold them in place." He took some not-so-sticky glue home and tried it out. Voilà! Those pieces of paper stuck to the hymnal page. Then, the big test: could he now remove the paper without damaging the hymnal page? **Double-voilà**!! They easily peeled off without leaving a mark.

Fry's tinkering transformed Spencer's glue into Post-it® Notes. Spencer was willing to *not know* how he could use his invention, and yet keep exploring. Fry was unsure how he'd fix that losing-my-place problem, but he kept exploring. So when you ask yourself, "Why should I push forward when I'm not sure what's going to happen?", then think of Post-it® Notes. Push into uncertain territory because that's the only way that new and surprising things can happen in your life. By the way, Spencer Silver's not-very-sticking Post-it® Notes have now taken in over $100 million from over 200 products.

"OK," you say. "Maybe it's worth it to try something new. But why should I do things that make me *uncomfortable*? That just seems plain stupid."

So, given that question, you might wonder why anyone in his or her right mind would choose to climb Mount Everest. This tallest mountain in the world stands 29,029 feet above sea level. At the top—the summit—the winds blow at hurricane force much of the year and the temperature averages 33 degrees below zero. There's only one-third the amount of oxygen in the air as there is at sea level. If you climb above 26,000 feet, **you'll need to breathe through tanks of oxygen**. You'll probably lose your appetite, get nauseous and even vomit. You'll feel dizzy lots of the time. Even at lower levels of the climb, you can get headaches and have shortness of breath.

You have to train for *one year* to get in condition to climb Mount Everest. Then it takes over *70 days* of climbing and resting to make it to the top. Anywhere along the way, fierce snowstorms can blow up unexpectedly, keeping you trapped for days. Avalanches are a constant threat. Any part of your body that is exposed to air can develop frostbite, which can permanently damage your skin.

Like Spencer Silver and Arthur Fry, Erik Weihenmayer [pronounced why-im-my-er] has had plenty of times where he didn't know how things would turn out. Added to that, he knows what real physical discomfort is. And he has endured it again and again for over two decades.

In 2001 he reached the summit of Mount Everest. By 2008 he climbed the last of the Seven Summits—the highest mountains on each of the world's seven continents. All that freezing cold, physical sickness, little sleep, low oxygen, snowstorms, potential avalanches. By achieving this tremendous feat of seven climbs, he joined an exclusive club of less than 100 mountaineers.

That's not all. In 2003, Erik completed the Primal Quest, a multi-sport race covering 457 miles through the Sierra Nevada Mountains. For six to ten days, teams bike, run, and whitewater paddle, averaging two hours of sleep per night. By the end, they will have pushed themselves up a total of 60,000 feet. That's **the height of *two* Mount Everests**, stacked up.

Erik is an awesome athlete. He's a master mountain climber, paraglider and skier. He has rock-climbed Yosemite National Park's El Capitan, a 3300-foot high overhanging rock wall. He has ice-climbed the 2600-foot Losar waterfall in the Himalaya Mountains of Nepal.

Oh, and, by the way, he has been blind since he was thirteen. So when he climbed 29,000 foot high Mount Everest, he was the first blind person in history to do that.

His commitment is so strong, there is very little Mother Nature can dish out that he is unwilling to adapt to. What drives him to suffer through extended periods of exhaustion, pain, and mental strain, weeks living out of a backpack, with no shower? He has dedicated his life to showing and teaching others that they can turn adversity into inner strength. Among his many contributions, he traveled to Tibet to teach the students of a school for the blind how to mountaineer and rock-climb. He took the teenagers on a climb 21,500 feet up Mount Everest, higher than any other team of blind people has attempted. You can rent the documentary of their feat. It's called "Blindsight," and it too is awesome and inspiring. I watched it in my den and when it was over, I jumped up and applauded! (Nobody saw me.)

Although Erik can't see, he has amazing vision. He imagines a world where people who have been labeled as weak, limited or incapable can **achieve more than anyone imagined**. He travels the world speaking, has written two great books and produced an award-winning film—all to convince people to take on daily struggles to reach their dreams.

Not Knowing, and Then Growing

I've got some advice for you. It will sound crazy when you read it. Nuts, really. But Mom and I have figured it out, and we've tried it out on ourselves, and taught it to Elliot, and gotten a few of my friends to try it.

We even taught it to some of our relatives. It works. Just like it worked for Silver and Fry and Weihenmayer [why-im-my-er]. Like it works for everyone who has achieved anything.

Here's what you do:

- Stop saying, "I've GOT to know that everything will turn out just right." Start saying, "I'm WILLING to NOT KNOW how things are going to turn out."
- Stop saying, "I've got to feel comfortable." Start saying, "I'm WILLING to feel UNCOMFORTABLE."

Then, while you're WILLING to not know and WILLING to feel uncomfortable, step into some unknown territory (you know, stuff you've been avoiding.)

You're probably thinking, "That's plain nuts!" (Didn't I tell you?) "Who on this planet would purposely choose to—be willing to—take some action when they might feel uncomfortable and unsure?"

Hmmm. How about Silver, Fry, and Erik Weihenmayer? What about all those great scientists, inventors, and authors that you've learned about in school? World-class athletes and musicians, or great leaders, like Martin Luther King, Jr.? Or those regular people, like Rosa Parks, who wouldn't give up her seat on the bus? Maybe your third grade teacher, or your cousin Tommy? Everyone who achieves anything great by trying new things has said to themselves, over and over, "I don't know how this is going to turn out, and I'm going to do it anyway."

And they've also said, over and over, "I'm willing to feel awkward, uncomfortable, clumsy. My goal is worth this effort." All the great people in the world—and a lot of regular people who have overcome their worries—have at least one trait in common: they are courageous. Everyone who has ever overcome an obstacle has shown courage. And you, fellow adventurer, can be courageous, too.

Here's the formula. Look at the conclusion.

BE WILLING TO FEEL UNSURE + BE WILLING TO FEEL UNCOMFORTABLE + STEP INTO THE UNKNOWN = COURAGE

Now, I'm pretty sure you don't have any immediate plans to climb Mt. Everest, so let's say you want to play outdoors... but you're worried that you might get stung by bees. Consider adopting this attitude:

"I'm willing to not know if I'm going to be stung."

Here comes the crazy talk again. Admit it. Get it out. **You think *I'm* crazy!** You're not going to read another word! In fact, you're going to **throw this book in the shower** and turn the water on!

Yeah, right. But wait a second. What if this approach works? It can't hurt to keep reading, can it? I'm not asking you to *do* anything (yet), just to consider some things. Hold off on that shower for a few more pages.

What if you absolutely, positively *must* know, *right* now, that you are going to eat a peanut butter and jelly sandwich for lunch tomorrow, starting exactly at 12:05 PM. I mean, you can't go on with life unless you know *right* now. Can you be sure? Of course you can't. If you decide you *must* know, *right* now, whether peanut butter will be sticking to the roof of your mouth at exactly 12:05 PM tomorrow, then how are you going to feel right now? Anxious. We can never know for sure what will happen in the future. We can make plans to increase the *chance* of things turning out. You can make that PB&J sandwich now (or, if you prefer, an asparagus-cheese-and-mustard dog...just wait until Chapter 9!) and put it in your book bag. You can set an alarm to go off at noon tomorrow so you'll be ready for 12:05. But you can't guarantee that the school won't have a fire drill just when you're ready to take that first bite.

So...when you are *willing* to be unsure, you are undoing your demand to know the unknown future. Trust me: this move is going to help you lots, once you learn it. We *can't* know the future. When we are willing to NOT know, we're now worried about one less thing. I'm not forgetting what it's like when you doubt that you can accomplish a task. When you are unsure how things are going to turn out, then you're going to feel uncomfortable, even anxious, as you get closer to doing that activity. You've got to be willing to be uncomfortable, too. Because if you're NOT willing to be uncomfortable, then you'll back away instead of move forward toward the activities that are important to you. When you're willing to be anxious (because you're unsure) while you try new things, then you have a better chance of pushing forward.

Why You Should Change Your Mind

Now you say, "Yes, kids have to be unsure and uncomfortable sometimes. But why-oh-why are you instructing me to be *willing* to be unsure and uncomfortable?" I'll tell you.

When you are willing to experience something that you think is going to be difficult, and when you're willing to not be sure you can accomplish it, here's what you get as a bonus:

- You're willing to keep going, even when you're not sure how things will turn out.
- You can handle any discomfort you might feel.
- Your brain comes up with creative ways to get through the task.
- Time seems to go by faster.

Put all that together, and what do you get? If you are willing to have doubts about how well you'll do, plus you're willing to feel anxious about those doubts, then it's all-around easier to handle new stuff.

It's not just adults who accomplish big things by doing this. Kids who do it accomplish even *small* things. Think back to the last chapter.

- Getting an injection at the doctor's. I decided to not know how shots are going to feel. I still don't *like* shots now, but I sure don't worry about them like I used to. Since I'm *willing* to not know how it's going to feel, I now have a creative way to handle my worries: I hear them like a chattering squirrel.
- Studying for a test. I wasn't sure I could learn the information, and I didn't know if I could pass the test. But I decided that was OK with me. So instead of worrying, I focused on what I needed to study. When my worries popped up, I talked back to them—"You're not helping. **I'm going to ignore you now**"—then concentrated on learning again.
- Getting to sleep at night. Kate decided it was OK for her worry to pop up and scare her at bedtime. So instead of trying to get rid of it, she cleverly imagined her worry as a scared rabbit with big brown eyes and a twitchy nose. She let it show up, but not take over her thoughts.
- Getting hit by a baseball. Elliot didn't *want* to get hit, but he realized it hardly ever happens, and if it *did* happen, he could handle it. That decision allowed him to concentrate on the fact that he *loves* playing baseball. And while he's up at bat, now he can concentrate on either hitting the ball or moving out of the way if it's a bad pitch. He's got more room in his mind to pay attention to his skills. And *that* makes it less likely that he'll get hit.

Here's a weird but true fact: when you spend less mental time worrying about bad things happening, you have a better chance to keep bad things from happening! Like Elliot: the less he *worried* about being hit, the more he could pay attention to his batting skills. That, of course, improved his chances of not being hit. Another one of Casey's weird but true facts (like the dazzle of Zebras.)

You haven't thrown the book in the shower yet ? I appreciate that. When I told you that you have to be uncomfortable and uncertain to grow in life, did you feel uncomfortable and unsure about what's next? And yet, you're still reading? Look at that! Progress already.

What's Next

Shall we continue? Next up...getting uncomfortable and uncertain on purpose, because that's how you reset your alarm system.

Chapter 7: Taking Your Brain for a Walk

It's time for a little brain talk. Not that you have a little brain. That's not what I meant. I'm sure your brain is perfectly sized. And I know it's busy. Boy, is it busy!

Anyway, your busy brain—and my brain and everybody else's brain—has a little structure in it that's shaped like an almond and is called the amygdala (which, by the way, means *almond*). You pronounce it this way: uh-MIG-duh-luh. Think of the amygdala as the brain's alarm center. It tells our body and mind to start taking care of us during emergencies. This is a very good thing.

Some families have a house alarm that will ring out at the sign of smoke or a break-in. In the same way, our brain's alarm center fires off when it thinks we are threatened. That's great! The amygdala automatically scares us when we see a snake, and prepares us to run away or freeze.

We all need an internal alarm that warns us of trouble. Even if your bike wheel slips for just a moment on a little sand, you'll feel that alarm run through your body within an instant. **It's *always* ready** to take care of you. If the tire had kept slipping on that sand and you risked falling off, your body would already be geared up **to help you catch your balance** again, since it responds to that prepare-for-danger button in three milliseconds. That's three one-hundredths of a second. Faster than a lightning strike.

What you *don't* need is a siren that goes off for no good reason. You don't want your house alarm to blare every time you make toast. You don't want the hotel sprinkler system to turn on every time other guests turn up the heat in *their* room. (OK, maybe that would be funny.) And you don't want your brain's alarm to scare you by mistakenly thinking that a belt is a snake, or to panic you each time you see the neighbor's friendly dog, or think about having fun with friends, or imagine any challenging adventure.

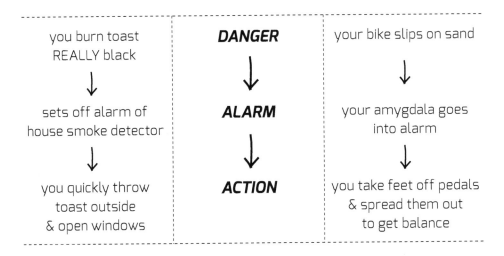

I'm going to make an educated guess here. Your amygdala—your alarm center—has been going off a little too frequently. That means you are feeling anxious when you may not need to be. For instance, if--when you were younger--you saw a lifeguard pull someone out of the ocean, you might have gotten quite scared during the event. Anyone would. But if somehow you then decide that swimming in the ocean, or swimming even in a pool, is full of risk, your alarm center may fire off every time you start thinking about going swimming.

When your alarm center has fired off a few times in a particular scene—like around the ocean or pool—it creates a set of automatic responses in your brain and body. Your typical pattern is probably to get worried, tense up about the possibility of something going wrong, and sometimes decide not to participate in the activity. Once that pattern is set in place, you can't simply switch it off like you can the house alarm.

Now, when you read this you're probably saying, "I can't switch it off? I *knew* there wasn't anything I could do! Why am I still reading this stupid book anyway? **Into the shower it goes**!" OK, calm down. Scientists have *proven*, without a doubt, that you can adjust your alarm if it sets off needlessly. I said we can't *switch* it off like we can a kitchen light, or the blender when we're creating home-made milk shakes. But we certainly *can* learn to turn it off, and we *will* succeed. *If* you really want to.

So, in Chapter 5 I taught you how to talk to your worry. How to handle it. How to be in charge of that worry part. Now I'm going to teach you how to talk to your amygdala, and how to handle those alarming body reactions that the amygdala sets off sometimes. To learn this, you will have to get uncomfortable and uncertain on purpose. (Come on, now. I warned you this was coming.)

You see, your amygdala needs to be retrained. It's gotten into some bad habits. And in order to retrain it, you need to have the **experience** of being uncomfortable and uncertain. You just can't retrain your amygdala by wishing it'll change from a distance. I'm sorry, but that's the truth.

It's like having a dog (let's call him Butch) who barks like crazy whenever he sees other dogs. Taking Butch for a walk is a challenge. He barks and jumps and pulls at the leash. But to retrain Butch to stop barking on his walks, he must **go for walks**. And see dogs. And learn not to react to them by barking. (My dog trainer friend says this involves a lot of cheese.)

My point is that you can't sit in your living room and hope that sometime in the future your amygdala will chill out whenever you enter new or uncomfortable situations. We need to take your amygdala out for a walk, and you, for obvious reasons, need to come along, too.

Think of our amygdala retraining program as a mental game. Your first challenge? To *stop* telling your alarm center to push the prepare-for-danger button (or "the danger button," for short). I'll teach you how to accomplish this, but it'll take you a little time. Got any spare time? Because if you'll play this game with me, then here's what you win: getting to do more fun things without worrying so much. Worth playing for?

So, how on earth are we going to help you to stop pressing your danger button? It's simple (not *easy*, but simple.). You're going to learn how to talk to your brain. Why? Because when you get scared, you say things that push that prepare-for-danger button. If you can stop telling your alarm center that there's danger, *it will learn on its own* not to push the prepare-for-danger button. Let me repeat, loudly:

YOU'RE GOING TO LEARN HOW TO TALK TO YOUR BRAIN.

Why?

BECAUSE YOU ARE PROBABLY SAYING THINGS THAT PUSH THAT DANGER BUTTON.

IF YOU WILL STOP TELLING YOUR ALARM CENTER THAT THERE'S DANGER, IT WILL LEARN ON ITS OWN NOT TO PUSH THAT DANGER BUTTON.

Your alarm center responds quickly and simply. It has only one task:

to protect you. It's a life-saver during true danger. But it takes all the fun out of other, non-dangerous times. Well, if the alarm center is trying to protect you, why does it keep pushing the danger button during non-dangerous times? Excellent question! Very important answer: because *you keep telling it that there is danger*! You can't flip the alarm *off* instantly, but you can flip it *on* in a flash. When you get scared about an event, you worry. When you worry, you say things like:

- "What if I have the same trouble as last time? I don't want that."
- "I could get anxious there. I don't want to be anxious. I want to feel relaxed."
- "I'm not going because I don't know how it's going to turn out."
- "Something bad could happen."
- "What if I get embarrassed? I can't handle that."
- "What if I get hurt? I don't want to get hurt."

When you worry like that, do you know what your alarm center hears? Only one thing: "Prepare for danger!" That's all it *can* hear. That's the only message that gets through. Your alarm center is powerful, but it's not a very sophisticated system. It doesn't have the ability to hear any of the details of your worries. It only picks up that one message: danger. It only has one button it can press: **prepare for danger**.

When I get scared and worried—no matter where I am or what I'm doing—I can hear myself ask for two things. See if you've heard these before:

- "I need to *know* how it's going to turn out."
- "I need to stop feeling anxious NOW!"

I'm learning to stop saying those unhelpful things as soon as I hear myself saying them. Then I replace them with, "I'm willing to not know how this turns out," and "I'm willing to feel anxious."

Here's an example. Let's pretend you're worried about flying on an airplane for the first time. Imagine a conversation between you and your amygdala (uh-MIG-duh-luh), the brain's alarm system.

(Wait. Hold on. I want to make sure you're clear on this very important point. When you're worried, and you think you're just talking to yourself in your mind, you're really not. Your amygdala is ALWAYS listening when you are scared. And it's ALWAYS going to respond by revving you up more. It's your biggest protector, and that's its only job. You call; it answers.)

So...back to the story. You start worrying big time about flying, and your amygdala triggers its alarm, just as it should.

> *You (talking to yourself)*: Oh, I don't know about this. I can't handle this. It's too much for me. I want to get out of here. I've never done this before.

> *Amygdala (listening in)*: What? We need to get out of here? Yikes. I'll get us ready. I'll get our heart beating, and our muscles ready to run. I'll rev up our body's engine.

> *You*: Well, now I'm feeling worse. My body isn't feeling right. That's too much. See! I knew I couldn't handle this. I really have to make it stop, but I can't. What is my body doing? Help!

> *Amygdala*: What's that? More panic messages! We need to get out of here, so let's crank it up! We're in danger, right? I'll do whatever you tell me to do.

> *You*: It's getting worse. I have to get out. My body feels terrible. I'm afraid of this airplane, and my body is out of control, too!

> *Amygdala*: Alarm system on! Danger!

> *You*: I can't handle this! What am I going to do?

Please understand that even though you don't know you're talking to your brain's alarm center, you are. Now let's try this same scene again: your first time on a plane. Watch what happens when you talk to yourself in a different way. You interrupt that "danger" message, and the alarm system turns back off.

You (talking to yourself): I'm not so sure about this. I've never done this before. Maybe this was a bad idea. Now I'm stuck on this plane, but I feel like I need to get out of here.

Amygdala (listening in): Wait, did you say *stuck*? Let's not be stuck. I'll get us ready to escape. Give me a half-second, and I'll get the alarm system going. All systems go.

You: Hey, now I feel bad! I'm all jittery. I don't like this!

Amygdala: That's my cue for action. **I'm here to save you**!

You: I've never done this plane thing before, so I don't know exactly how it's going to go. I'm nervous, and I can feel my body being nervous, too. But I really *want* to go on this flight. Driving to Florida takes so much longer. I'm nervous, but I can handle this. I can handle feeling uncomfortable. I want to get to Florida, so I want to fly on this plane. If I *have* to feel uncomfortable to get through it, then I'm willing to feel uncomfortable.

Amygdala: So now you're saying you want to stay on the airplane? Oh, great. I've already set the alarm system in motion. I'm already preparing for the escape. Now what?

You: Well, listen to me when I tell you that this is really fine. I feel uncomfortable, but it's not an unexpected emergency. It's so easy to set you off, Amygdala, but I'm working on changing that. Once we move through these sensations together, the next time will be a bit easier.

Amygdala: Really? It's just that I've gotten used to jumping into action so quickly…You mean this isn't quite so serious? Here, I'll turn down the juice. See if this is what you want.

You: OK, good. I feel a bit better already. Now I'm just going
to breathe a bit. No escape needed. I can expect to feel
uncomfortable here. It's part of the process. Heart beating a bit,
butterflies in my stomach. But certainly not an emergency.

Amygdala: You seem to be handling this, so I can keep the major
alarm system off. I'm clear now that you're telling me this is just
a new experience for you, but not an emergency. I'll keep you in
"new experience" mode of arousal.

You: Whew! That was close. I was feeling pretty uncomfortable for a
bit. We got through it, though, didn't we?

Amygdala: We did, alright. I'll stay in touch. Now fasten your seat
belt.

See the difference? In the first conversation, when you start to worry
big time, the brain's amygdala does what it's trained to do: it sets off its
alarm system. Then you start freaking out because the alarm system is
going off. Body tight. Engine racing.

In the second conversation, you expect to have some worries and
be uncomfortable. But you remind yourself (remember, the amygdala
is listening) of this important fact: while being uncomfortable and
uncertain is a normal part of this new situation, setting off a serious
alarm response is not necessary. You slow down those racing thoughts,
and you send different messages to your alarm center. The amygdala
decides, "I can take this down a notch. It's not a crisis."

When you stop sending out those very unhelpful messages (and
that's our plan), you stop telling your alarm center to press the prepare-
for-danger button. Once your alarm system calms down, you can start
learning new things. When you hear yourself saying, "I have to know
how everything's going to turn out" or "I have to feel calm," then you can
change those messages to "I'm willing..." And what are you willing to

do? You're willing to be unsure and uncomfortable.

If that's not clear to you, let's review:

All of us must face two tasks in order to reach new and difficult goals. It's true for me, for you, for our friends. It's true for our parents, teachers, aunts and uncles. It's true for everyone who's ever walked the earth.

- We have to feel unsure.
- We have to feel uncomfortable about feeling unsure.

When we try new things, we can't be sure how they will turn out. Is it worth it? Thomas Edison thought so. They say he **failed over 6000 times**, and refused to give up, until he finally perfected the first electric light bulb. His biggest struggle? He needed to invent a special kind of filament for the bulb. He sent men to South America, Jamaica, China, Japan, and Ceylon (now Sri Lanka) and Burma (now Myanmar) in Asia to search for just the right thread, and couldn't find it. He finally discovered the correct fiber and spent days preparing it. Then, it broke just as he transferred it to the bulb. He immediately worked another 48 hours without sleep to prepare a second thread. When a reporter asked him why he continued when he had failed so many times, he replied, "I have not failed but have successfully discovered 6000 ways that won't work!" That's persistence.

You are no different than Silver or Fry (the Post-it® Notes guys) or Erik (the blind mountain climber) or Edison. You can reach your goals just like they reached theirs. Their only advantage was that they were willing to be uncertain and uncomfortable and push forward anyway. They grabbed hold of their courage and pulled themselves into the unknown.

You *can* succeed. And you will. If you train. Like Butch.

Stepping into It on Purpose

Can we teach Butch to handle other dogs without actually taking him around other dogs? No. He has to see them, smell them, hear them, and learn to respond differently. You, courageous reader, must do the same, by moving forward into your new activities.

The first step is to talk differently to your alarm center so that you stop pressing the danger button. These are the messages you need to try out, little by little:

"I'm willing to feel uncomfortable."

"I'm willing to feel unsure, and to not know what will happen."

"I'm willing to grab onto my courage and *do it*."

The second step—more of a big leap, actually—is to walk into unfamiliar situations, or situations that have scared you before (but aren't truly dangerous). You need to take small steps toward the activities you've been backing away from. And do that voluntarily, *on purpose*.

Why do this? Because....

- You want to be less afraid in certain situations, right?
- You'll get to participate in more activities that aren't truly dangerous.

Remember, your alarm center has been trained to automatically push the prepare-for-danger button when you get close to things that scared you in the past. That means *for a while*, even if you decide that you want to participate in those activities, you'll *keep* feeling uncertain and anxious (because the prepare-for-danger button fires off automatically now.)

Do you want to go forward? Do you want to learn how to handle the events that make you nervous? That REQUIRES that you feel unsure and uncomfortable, just as Butch's retraining requires that he see other dogs on his walks. You can *fight* those feelings, but they're coming anyway. Fighting them makes you more uncomfortable.

Here's my coaching: do just the opposite of trying to be sure and comfortable. That's the next piece of our puzzle: BE *UN*SURE AND *UN*COMFORTABLE ON PURPOSE.

be unsure &
uncomfortable
ON PURPOSE

Wow! Who in the world would choose to do that!! Oh, yeah, remember who? All the great leaders in the world, ever. All the great thinkers and painters and athletes. All kids and grownups, throughout history, who have ever overcome their fears. That's a lot of people. If they've done it, and I've done it, I KNOW you can do it.

Let's say that you've been afraid to sit in the cafeteria with other kids. You've been saying to yourself, "That would be terrible. I'm too uncomfortable to do that. They're going to hate me…. Please make this end!" Now you want to overcome this fear, tough as it seems. Here's how you begin:

IF

you will talk with other kids in the cafeteria, especially while you are uncomfortable

AND IF

you can think-&-believe something like, "This is hard, and I'm *willing* to do it because it will help me get stronger here,"

THEN

your alarm center can begin learning that sitting in the cafeteria with other kids is relatively safe.

That's what you do the *first* time. Look what happens if you repeat it.

IF

you *keep* talking to kids in the cafeteria, day after day

THEN

your alarm center will learn that it doesn't need to automatically press the danger button when you sit with other kids in the cafeteria

THEN

you will start feeling less anxious as you head into the cafeteria

This works the same way in *any* hard situations:

IF

you can stay in difficult situations by thinking-&-believing, "This might be hard, but I'm willing to do it so I can get stronger here"

AND STOP SAYING

"This is terrible. I hate this. I don't want to do this. Things could go terribly wrong here..."

THEN

your alarm center can start to learn that this event is relatively safe

That's how it goes the *first* time. Here's what happens over time.

WHEN

you willingly repeat that experience many times

THEN

your alarm center will learn that it doesn't need to automatically press the danger button when you enter that situation

THEN

you will stop being so anxious as you head into the situation

Are you with me?

So…the best way to reverse this process of being frightened and worried (and reset that amygdala) is to *stop* saying, "I don't want this" (which pushes the danger button) and *start* saying, "I'm willing…"

And then take some action!

Here's how this stance might sound:

- "I'm going to play outdoors. And I'm willing to not know if I'll be stung by a bee."
- "I'm going to learn to play the guitar. And I'm willing to feel anxious about sounding terrible and being laughed at."
- "I'm going to try out for cheerleading. And I'm willing to not know if they'll accept me."
- "I'm going to spend the night at my friend's house. And I'm willing to not know if I'll get scared and have to come home."
- "When I try new things and I don't know how they're going to turn out, I tend to get anxious. Since I want to try new things, then I'm willing to get anxious."

I've been practicing this for over a year now, and I can tell you that there are some great advantages. I'm more motivated. My first worries still pop up, but I can pull myself past them. I'm not always fighting against myself. So I'm more focused on my task.

And there's more that I've gained as I continue to practice like this:

- I don't mind being uncomfortable, as long as I'm learning to do something I want to do.
- I can let myself be doubtful about how things are going to turn out.
- I find new and clever ways to reach my goals.
- I stop pushing the prepare-for-danger button, so I end up less anxious.
- When I explore new territory, I learn. When I learn, I grow. I *want* to grow.

How would you like to say that about the adventures in *your* life? Let's get you there!

What's Next?

We're going to talk more about this idea of being unsure and uncomfortable on purpose. You'll need a lot of motivation and a few important tools so you can feel scared and still keep moving forward. I'm here to help with the motivation and the tools.

I've talked a lot about getting uncomfortable. Feeling anxious. Handling those uncomfortable sensations. Even doing things to produce them, for goodness sake. I'm going to go out on a limb here—a short limb, actually—and predict what you might be thinking about all of my "uncomfortable" talk. Maybe something like this?

"So, Casey says I need to feel *uncomfortable*. When I have to [*fill in the blank with something you don't like to do, like getting an injection or trying out for the soccer team*], I don't feel uncomfortable, I feel downright *miserable*! My body does some very funky things. I start shaking and feel like I'm going to barf. What am I supposed to do about *that*?"

Excellent question. I've given you some enormously helpful (if I do say so myself) information about managing your thoughts. And about changing the way you talk to worry and your alarm system. But there's another important topic to cover. Based on my experience, and after hearing the stories of lots of other kids, I think we focus *a lot* on all the bad sensations in our bodies. Therefore…I've got a couple tricks to help you *handle* those anxious sensations. This will make it easier for you to retrain your brain. Just me, being helpful. Shall we continue?

Chapter 8: I Say Uncomfortable, You Say Vomit

Last weekend, I went to an amusement park with my friend Lindsay. It's only about an hour from my house, so we go every summer. The park has kiddie rides like carousels and those little boats that float around in a circle. And it has crazy rides that twist and spin upside down. And then there's **the Yankee Cannonball**. It's a classic wooden roller coaster built in 1934. The ride lasts one minute and fifty-two seconds from start to finish. It has steep hills and banked curves. It's scary, and it's awesome. Until last weekend, I'd always watched other kids ride it, wishing I could get up the nerve to ride it myself. Then I did. Get up the nerve, that is.

We stood in line for twenty minutes, which is typical for that very popular ride. My heart was beating faster than normal. My armpits were sweating. I kept jumping up and down in place because I felt like I had to *move* my body. It was like having jolts of extra energy running through my veins.

Gripping onto Fun

Like most roller coasters, the Yankee Cannonball started with a long, slow climb up a very steep track. The wheels were clacking along, and gravity was pressing my back against the seat. My heart pounded. I gripped the bar in front of me, just to keep my hands from shaking like a Chihuahua in the freezing rain. I bounced my legs up and down, and I seemed to alternate between holding my breath and panting like that Chihuahua. Right then, I panicked. I turned to my friend Lindsey. She was scrunched in next to me. "This is crazy. I'm going to puke!"

And there was Lindsay (who doesn't worry much at all), gripping the bar with *her* hands, and bouncing *her* legs, with eyes wide open and lips pursed up tight. "This is how they build the tension!" she yelled over the clacking wheels. "When we go over the top, **let your body go loooose! And scream**!"

Really. Like she had to *tell* me to scream. Please.

Let my body go loose? That was something I'd heard before. Something I'd even practiced. Until Lindsay said that, I didn't even consider doing it on a roller coaster. As we went over the top of the first big hill, I actually listened to her, and let my body get looser. I sat in that seat, and I let myself move whatever way the coaster and gravity and speed made me move. We screamed a bunch over the next minute-and-a-half, and my heart still raced as we came to a stop, but I didn't fight the roller coaster at all once I decided to let loose and scream. I allowed my body to go with it. I even laughed.

We went again, and then a third time. We screamed and laughed louder each time.

Of course, there's a reason I'm telling you this story. (I love when I learn something from my experiences and can share it with you.) On the way home from the amusement park that day, when we were quiet and a bit tired in the car, I analyzed my roller coaster ride.

How did I do it? How did I have fun? **How did I *not* puke**?

I certainly didn't feel calm while we were in line or while we crept up that first big hill. I was excited, and I was nervous. OK, I was even *scared.* I wanted to go on that roller coaster, and I hoped it would be fun, but I really didn't know if I'd like it.

How did I go from being scared to having fun? I didn't let my nervousness and my uncertainty *trigger my alarm system.* While I waited in line, I reminded myself that my feelings were normal. I was excited *and* nervous! When I looked around at the other people in line with us, they seemed to be acting the same way I was. I could feel the energy in that line. And as we climbed up that hill, I saw Lindsay—non-worrying Lindsay—doing the same things I was doing.

And then Lindsay told me to *go loose.* Could it be that simple? Kind of, actually. Our bodies will react to being afraid. When your body *starts* to react, you, of course, can do things to make it oh-so-much worse. You can also do things to make it slow down or hold steady. One of those things is to get physically loose and relaxed. It's not possible to be relaxed and freaked out at the same time. Your fight-or-flight system gets you ready to fight or run away. When you loosen your body, you send the opposite message. When muscles relax, your body and brain are not yelling, "Danger!" Loose and dangerous? Relaxed and panicked? It just doesn't happen that way.

I learned about this long before Lindsay reminded me on the roller coaster. A year ago I talked to an expert on worry and what it does in our bodies. He showed me a quick experiment. (You should try it for yourself.)

"Okay, Casey, hold this pencil for me, by making a fist, like you were holding the handle of a tennis racket or an umbrella. Now squeeze the pencil as hard as you can. Really squeeze it hard, so your fingers get tired and even the muscles in your arm are working. Keep it up! Really squeeze tight! Now, keep squeezing…but at the same time, loosen your fingers so the pencil drops. That's right…squeeze sooo tightly, but relax, too, and drop the pencil."

Get it? I couldn't do it. You can't do it either. Try it. I'll wait.

See what I mean? And see why you need to understand that you can't be tight and loose at the same time? It means that you can *immediately* begin to turn your alarm system off by shifting from tight to loose. This really helped me feel better equipped as I set out to be unsure and uncomfortable, so I want to give you some specifics about this piece of the puzzle.

Cooling Out

Someone once told me that when her panicky feelings started, she gave up control and just had to let them go on and on until the episode ended. I don't believe that at all, and you shouldn't either. I realize, of course, that you're still learning to become an **experienced worry manager**, and if you practice some of these new ways of thinking and responding, you might set off your alarm system. After all, I'm telling you to go *into* the situations that make you worried and scared, and to practice getting uncomfortable. So, even though the goal is to retrain your brain and quiet down that alarm, let's be realistic: it might go off. If the panicky feelings and sensations start up, you need ways to help manage them.

One way is to change how you talk to yourself in those moments, to first remind yourself that this isn't an emergency and tell yourself that you can handle these uncomfortable sensations. Of course, you can't say you can handle your feelings unless you have experience successfully handling them. You'd never say, "*I can* ride a *unicycle* down three staircases while balancing a *basketball* on the end of my finger!" (unless you really could). In that same way, I'm going to coach you how to calm your body down, so you'll be able to say, "I know how to calm myself down," and really mean it. And it'll be **easier** to learn **than that**

unicycle-basketball thing.

My mom and I discovered some breathing and relaxation skills that helped me calm my body and quiet my mind. We found ones made for grown-ups, so we decided to change some things up to make them more kid-friendly (the grown-up stuff was a *little* slow). I wrote our new instructions down, practiced reading them and then recorded them onto my iPod so I could listen to them as often as I wanted.

The original instructions said to practice when you *weren't* in the middle of a problem. In other words, don't wait until you *need* to calm down to *learn* to calm down. That made sense to us. Our town fire department practices putting out fires in a big empty parking lot behind the station. They don't wait to test out the equipment when someone's house is on fire. They're **too busy putting out the fire** (of course). So I started practicing these skills during times when I *wasn't* pressing the panic button.

And this is cool: I kept practicing until I got really good at using the techniques, so now it's so much easier to calm down when I want to. Since I know they work as soon as I need them, I feel prepared when I'm going into new, scary situations. And because I feel prepared, I hardly ever *need* to use them anymore. Now I usually just remind myself that I can handle being nervous, and I move forward. But if I start getting a little overwhelmed, I pull out my calming skills.

In the beginning I practiced the skills and I used them often. You should do the same. Later—after they've helped you out of a bunch of jams—I'll bet you'll be like me and you won't have to use them much.

There are a couple of breathing skills that I still use lots. Why? Because they remind me that I can handle what's going on right now. Like today in American history class, Mr. Nelson said, "OK, everybody, get out your pencils for a pop quiz on what you read last night." Now, I did read the chapter last night. But I had music playing, and Boo kept jumping up on the bed and rubbing onto me and doing his purring thing. So all of a sudden, as I heard Mr. Nelson say that, I thought that maybe I didn't concentrate that well last night. Right then and there I took a Calming Breath (that's what Mom and I call it). When you calm your breathing, you send your body the "I can handle this" message, not the "emergency" message. Then you can move forward without so much trouble. That's what I did. I took that Calming Breath and, like always (because I've practiced it a gazillon times), I quieted down and stopped scaring myself. Then I could concentrate on the quiz.

I'm not saying I got a perfect score. But I did better than I would have if I tried to remember what I read and simultaneously thought, "Oh, no! I'm not ready! Why didn't I concentrate last night! If I do badly on this, I'll be so embarrassed!"

So this is a good spot to add the next piece to our puzzle. This one's easy to remember: BREATHE!

It'll take you about 30 seconds to take a Calming Breath. I've written it out for you here. If you've got 30 seconds to spare, give it a try. I'll wait.

Calming Breath

1. Breathe out all the way.
2. Take a deep breath in, letting your belly expand first, and then your chest.

3. Slowly exhale, saying "calm" (or a similar word) under your breath. (I say "okay" to myself, or sometimes I say, "fine." I keep it simple.)
4. Let your muscles go limp & warm; loosen your face & jaw muscles.
5. Remain in this "resting" position for a few more seconds, without thinking about your breathing or anything else.

When I have a lot of racing thoughts and I'm having trouble quieting them down, then I turn to Calming Counts, because Calming Counts takes about 90 seconds instead of 30 seconds. During that minute-and-a-half, I have to concentrate on all the steps of the exercise. That's good. Why? Because when I'm concentrating on the steps of the breathing skill, I can't also be worrying. So Calming Counts helps me in two ways. It helps me feel more physically relaxed and it pulls my attention away from the not-so-helpful thoughts that are scaring me. Then, when I've calmed down a little, I can easily say, "Those thoughts aren't helpful; I'm letting them go." A reset.

Calming Counts
1. Breathe out all the way.
2. Take a deep breath in, letting your belly expand first, and then your chest.
3. Slowly exhale, saying "calm" (or some other simple word) under your breath.
4. Now take ten gentle, easy breaths, while you silently count down with each exhale, starting with "ten."
5. At the same time, invite the muscles in your jaw or forehead or stomach to loosen. Imagine them loosening.

See what I mean? You just focus on taking ten easy, loose, gentle breaths while giving a calming message to you entire body and brain. Sometimes, while I'm counting down and getting loose, I smile to myself. Breathe. Loose. Smile. So cool!

How Not to Do It Bridget's Way

There's an important point I need to go over with you. Some of you might be asking, "Is Casey telling me two different things. In Chapter 6 she tells me to *be willing to get uncomfortable.* Now she's telling me to calm myself and make my body loose. Which is it? Be uncomfortable? Or be relaxed?"

Well...both. I want you to be able to manage your body's reactions so your alarm system quiets down. And I want you to step into those scary, new situations. When any of us steps into such situations, we'll feel uncomfortable for a while. When that happens to you, I want you to be *willing* to be uncomfortable and to know that you can handle those uncomfortable sensations without freaking out and making them worse. Understanding what's happening, taking some nice Calming Breaths, loosening your muscles, and talking to yourself differently...these all slow down the alarm system.

Feeling uncomfortable is NOT the same as setting off your alarm system. Guess what? It all depends on what you say when you start feeling uncomfortable.

Let me give you an example. I run on the cross-country team at school. I'm not super-fast, but we have fun. Most of our races are about three miles long. My friend Bridget is also on the team. **She's much faster** than I am...**when she's not freaking out**.

I often learn about how to manage my worry by watching other people, and Bridget, without even knowing it, has kindly shown me what NOT to do. Over and over.

It goes like this: We have cross-country races with other schools, and each race is called a "meet." We're supposed to arrive for a meet about an hour before the start time. We warm up, stretch, drink water. We chatter a lot and move around because most of us have some nervous energy inside. Bridget gets there with the rest of us, and she does okay for the first half hour or so. But then she starts pacing and shaking her hands like she's trying to get slime off them. With about fifteen minutes to go before the start, she begins saying, "I feel sick. I'm going to throw up. I hate throwing up. I feel nauseous. Oh, not again. I can't handle throwing up." She goes on and on like this, and it gets worse as we approach the start of the race. She tells everyone how she *hates* to throw up, how she's *going* to throw up, how she will *die* if she throws up! (She has thrown up a few times, by the way. She lived.)

The race starts, and we all run as best we can. Most of us push ourselves during those three miles, and we're pretty spent at the end of the race. That's when Bridget starts in again. "I'm going to puke. I feel so *awful*. I *hate* this. If I puke, **I'm going to *freak out*!**" She often cries. And freaks out.

When I watch Bridget, I say to myself, "That's how to set off your alarm system, right there."

The truth is, I often feel a little nauseous before a meet. I get nervous. My stomach feels jumpy. I usually don't want to eat breakfast in the morning before the meet. And do I feel a little sick when I finish? I think everyone on the team does at times. It's worse when it's hot out, or when I push myself at the end to catch somebody on the other team.

But I am *not* setting off my alarm system. I'm *not*. While I'm getting ready before the race and feeling queasy, I walk around and take some nice Calming Breaths. Sometimes I lie on the grass and focus on gravity, letting my muscles sink into the ground. My nervousness doesn't completely go away (it's normal, of course), but it stays at a manageable level. At the end of the race, when I actually feel like I could puke, I've learned to walk and breathe and imagine my heart slowing down gradually. I can feel it happening in my chest. And I say to myself, "Hey, I don't like puking either, but I can handle it. It might happen, but I'm going to help my body calm down. I feel kinda gross but I'm okay."

What's Next

I have fun at my cross-country races. Sure, I feel uncertain sometimes, and tired, and even downright gross when I finish. But I also laugh with my friends and cheer on my teammates. I've made some new friends and I've improved my times this year. All of this makes me feel great. My worry, if it were in charge, might have stopped me from joining the team and going to the meets. I want to be a part of that whole experience. I want to get faster and have fun. Maybe by the time I graduate from high school, I'll win a race. I'm sure I'll set a new personal record by then. I want to keep going, and having a **want to** is what the next chapter is all about.

A *want to* is what keeps you moving forward, even when you hit a tough challenge, or an uncomfortable sensation, or a worried thought. Or when your mom makes you eat canned asparagus. Or you have to jump out of a helicopter. Curious? Good. Turn the page. A key element of the plan is about to be revealed.

Chapter 9: Wrestling with Asparagus

Benjamin and his uncle Steve taught me some amazing things about worry…ways of handling worry that I never even considered. Have you ever watched the trailers at the movies, and the guy with the low booming voice says, "**After this movie, you'll never look at [*fill in the blank*] the same way again!**" That's what I'm saying to you right now: I don't think I'll ever again get out-maneuvered by worry like I used to.

When I met Benjamin, he was almost thirteen years old. We were taking the same art class last summer. Benjamin, like me, was a conversationalist, so we talked while we painted and sculpted and cleaned up, and I figured out pretty quickly that we had some things in common. One day I asked him if he wanted to come over after class and maybe go swimming at my neighbor's pool. He said yes almost before I finished the invitation. Then, in typical Benjamin fashion, he said quite a bit more.

"You know, a few years ago, I would have never come over to your house. I would have made up some excuse, like my mom wouldn't let me, or I had to go somewhere. When I was around ten I started having a real problem going to other kids' houses. It was weird. I'd start to think about going, and I'd really want to go because it sounded fun and everything, but then I'd start worrying about stuff. What if I was hungry and they didn't have any food I liked? What if I got bored but my mom wasn't coming back for two hours? What if the dad was mean? What if the house smelled weird? Then I'd tell myself that it was easier to stay home because there was just too much I didn't know, and my house was perfectly fine. I stayed that way for a while."

I asked him what happened. How did he fix it? What changed?

"Uncle Steve took me fishing. Maybe my parents and Uncle Steve planned it, so Steve could talk to me about my worry. I'm not sure. But while we fished, he told me a few things that made a big difference. A huge difference."

Remember the day I met the girl in the doctor's office? I think I had the same look on my face. I was staring and nodding, with very little blinking. "AND?"

"Uncle Steve is in the Coast Guard. He rescues people at sea when boats sink or get lost in a storm. He and his team of rescuers go on searches in a helicopter, right into a storm. And when they find people in trouble, he gets lowered out of the helicopter into the waves. Sometimes he jumps. It's risky, and so I always just assumed that he was the bravest guy ever. No worries for Uncle Steve!"

(Can you imagine me staring and nodding? I don't even think I was breathing that much.)

"But Uncle Steve told me that when he started his training, he wondered if he'd make it through. It was tough. He was wet and cold and sick to his stomach, and thirsty and tired and sore. Almost every part of that early training made him uncomfortable in some way, and that's probably putting it mildly.

"Then it got worse. He had always dreamed of being in the Coast Guard because he loved the ocean and boats, but he discovered he was very worried about flying in a helicopter. So when they first told him he qualified to be a rescue swimmer—and that meant **jumping out of a helicopter into the stormy water**—he wanted to quit. Not just flying in a helicopter, but then jumping out of one! He was freaking out!"

"Really, Benjamin," I clarified, "jumping out of a helicopter into the ocean during a storm is a lot different than going over to a friend's house."

Benjamin laughed out loud. "I know that!" he answered, still laughing. "But Uncle Steve showed me how our worries were alike. First, he said, we both wanted to do something that was important to us. Second, we both knew that avoiding the scary stuff would make us feel better right away. He imagined quitting the Coast Guard, and I thought about the comfort of staying home. By quitting and giving up, our worries would be gone, wouldn't they? Or so we told ourselves."

(Me, nodding.)

"But Uncle Steve told me how much he wanted to get into the Coast Guard. It was his goal since high school. When he thought about quitting, he knew it was a way to stop being scared, but it wasn't what he truly wanted. Going to friends' houses and being a part of the fun was really important to me, too. Staying home and refusing invitations made me comfortable for that moment, but it didn't get me what I wanted in the long run. I didn't want to be left out."

As I'm sure you know, when you feel scared, it's very hard to let yourself keep feeling scared. You want to stop it, so usually you back away from whatever's scaring you. To keep going, you must have a goal you want to reach. Because when you stand face-to-face with your fear, you have to see over to the other side of it, to what your life will be like when you get past your fear.

This brings us to the next piece of the puzzle: KNOW WHAT YOU WANT.

KNOW what you want

Kate, Elliot, Benjamin and his uncle Steve each had a want. And it *motivated* them to face what they feared.

- Kate wanted to fall asleep at night without being so afraid and without her parents in her room. So she wanted to stay in her bed and practice feeling scared.
- Elliot wanted to hit the baseball and win baseball games. So he was willing to get up to bat and swing, knowing he might get hit by the ball.
- Benjamin wanted to be included with his friends. You'll soon find out what that desire motivated him to do.
- Uncle Steve wanted to get into the Coast Guard. Wait 'til you hear what he does to face his fear.

When we know what we want—and we really want it—then it motivates us to do the hard stuff. Really wanting something can give us courage. If you think back on all the stories I've told you, this is a common theme.

Chapter 1
- I wanted to feel safe riding my bike.
- I wanted to handle walking past that dog on the way to the school bus stop.

Chapter 4

- I wanted to enjoy the water park with my friends.

Chapter 5

- That girl at the doctor's office wanted to handle getting injections.
- And so did I.
- Mom wanted to pace herself so that she wouldn't be overwhelmed with too many duties.
- I wanted to do well on the math test.

Chapter 6

- Spencer Silver wanted his invention of not-so-sticky glue to be useful.
- Arthur Fry wanted his hymnal markers to stay in place.
- Erik Weihenmayer still wants to show people who feel limited that they can achieve more than they ever imagined.

Chapter 8

- I wanted to ride the Yankee Cannonball with Lindsay.
- I wanted to run (and maybe win!) at my crosscountry meets.

What do you want? If you decide to want something *strongly enough*, then you're going to find the courage to face the hard stuff that might stand between you and your goal. Do you remember the definition of courage? To be scared and do it anyway.

OK, back to Benjamin's story. Benjamin's uncle Steve imagined himself in the Coast Guard, and he was excited about the idea. He was determined to get there. So he figured out how to handle his worries. Listen up, because he used the same little tricks that I've been teaching you. See if you notice.

"Hang On… We're Going In!"

"Uncle Steve could see from those first few months of training that being new in the Coast Guard meant that he was going to be uncomfortable. He also figured out that when it was time to jump out of that helicopter—when he was standing in the open door, looking at the water and feeling the wind—his uncomfortable worry would be right there with him. There was no way around it. So he invited it along. He *welcomed* it. He told himself that in order to be a good rescue swimmer, he had to feel uncomfortable. The more uncomfortable he felt, the better his training was going.

"When the helicopter took off, and his stomach leapt like he was on a roller coaster, he said, '**Great! This is what I need**!' When the doors opened and he looked down at the choppy water, and his heart raced and his feet felt heavy, he said, 'More, please!' When he leaned over the edge and threw up, he said, '**Bring it on**!' And when it was time to practice going into the water, he said to his worry, 'Hang on, we're going in!' He told me all this as we fished and ate our sandwiches. I had no idea! He was brave, alright, but it wasn't because he didn't worry. It was because he kept his worry right there with him even though he felt terrible at times. He really wanted to finish his training, so he had to invite his worry along instead of fighting against it."

After Benjamin spent the day with his uncle, he decided to give this approach a try. He knew he wanted to go to his friends' houses. No doubt about that. He practiced what he would say when an invitation came. He even wrote it down and kept it in his pocket. It went something like this:

"Hey, worry, we've just been invited to Jason's house. Let's go. Yeah, you're coming with me. I want you to come. I WANT YOU TO BE THERE. I, in fact, wouldn't think of going without you. I'm going to learn to deal with you, so give me something to work with, would you?

No more avoiding. We're going in, so bring it on!" (He took that last line from Uncle Steve because it sounded so cool.)

When the next invitation came, the worry showed up, as expected. One morning at school, his friend Jason said, "Hey, do you want to come over after school?" Benjamin quickly said, "Yes, I do want to. I really do want to." Three times during the day he pulled out his paper and read it over a few times. After school, as Benjamin walked over to Jason's house, worry came along, as instructed. (The paper was still in his pocket.) After hanging out at Jason's house for about 20 minutes, Benjamin felt okay, not great. But he still stayed for another hour before he walked home. Then he called Uncle Steve. "Training underway." That was the message he left on Steve's voice mail. How awesome is that?

Remember that piece of the puzzle in Chapter 7? "Be unsure and uncomfortable on purpose." I admit that it does sound strange. But once you understand the benefit of this attitude, things will change for you in a big way, as they changed for Uncle Steve and Benjamin. Uncle Steve taught Benjamin how to **invite worry**, to **make it a part of the training**. Why? Because Benjamin *knew* he wanted to hang out at his friends' houses. If he was going to try that, he was going to have to be okay with not knowing how it would turn out. When you know what you want and you're determined to get it, then you'll be willing to put up with some hard times.

Uncle Steve could teach him that because he'd already done it himself. He knew what he wanted more than anything: to join the Coast Guard. And he knew that if he was going to reach his goal, there was no magic pill to get rid of his worries; they were going to be *part* of his training. Standing in that helicopter, he showed us how feeling worried and uncomfortable moved him closer to his goal. He expected. He worried. He externalized. He talked. And then he wanted to do it over and over. On purpose!

Let me review. Worry *must* show up if you want to learn a new way to manage it. Trying new things is a good way to get it to show up. You'll feel more motivated to face your worries if you pick things that you really want to accomplish.

I understand that this is a new concept for you. Even though you might be saying, "Huh?" to yourself, and feeling a bit confused, keep going. I have more explaining to do.

Wrestling with Asparagus

Sometimes some things work out perfectly. That's what's happened in our neighborhood. We've lived in our house my whole life, and we've always had a pretty okay street. But in the summer before sixth grade, two new families moved in, and then everything changed. There were now just enough boys for Elliot and just enough girls for me. We had spend-the-night parties with movies in the Palmatier's back yard. Kickball games in the field across the street. Arguments didn't last long and the neighborhood parents seemed to act like we were *all* their kids. It was easy to run in and out of everybody's houses.

I tell you this because something happened that's really important to our project here. Last fall, we scheduled our neighborhood club meeting on a Sunday afternoon in the O'Donnell's basement. Why the basement? Because Sara and Adrian's dad volunteered to help us start building a clubhouse there and then move it into their back yard. I couldn't wait! Then the trouble began.

At our Sunday dinner, Mom serves up the usual stuff, with one exception: asparagus. Not your normal, buy-a-bunch-of-asparagus-and-steam-it-up-and-serve-it-with-butter asparagus. No, she buys *canned* asparagus. You've probably never had the pleasure of meeting canned asparagus, so let me introduce you. **It's soft. Mushy, even. Slimy.**

Gag-able.

"Forget it," I say. "I'm not eating this. It's gross." My bad. Mom decides to take this as a personal insult, and the standoff begins. "The only way you're going to the club meeting is if you finish all that asparagus." Elliot, who thinks this is all too funny, pops his in the microwave, gets it all steamy and hot, and slides it down quickly. Me? I'm cutting off the tiniest tip of one, starring at it on the end of my fork, and gagging as I put it in my mouth.

I can't do it. I can't eat this slime. I make some more gagging sounds. I cry. Tick, tick, tick. I get *really* mad. I negotiate. But there I sit. Tick, tick, tick, tick. Forty-five minutes. I want *so badly* to be part of that building project today. I can't *imagine* missing out on it. But I'm repulsed by the green slime. I *can't* eat it.

Then. Suddenly. Up pops a message in my brain. I have no idea where it came from, but I can still hear that voice in my head. "I *want* to eat that asparagus." Just as suddenly I jump up from the table, grab a hotdog bun from the fridge, open it up wide, lay the asparagus in, put some cheese on top, and pop it in the toaster oven. When it's done, I slap some mustard on top, fold it over, and **down the whole asparagus-dog without a flinch**. Out the door I run, off to help build the best clubhouse a neighborhood could ever want.

Is that weird or what?! I really don't know how that thought showed up in my mind, but I can tell you this: it has changed my life. Honest. Now when I get afraid and stuck, if I can remember what I learned that day last fall, I can figure how to get unstuck.

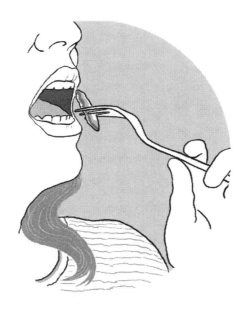

Now I see it as a game I play with my worries. Here's how my game strategy worked that day, and how it can work for you. It's really quite logical, in a twisted sort of way. I wanted to get to that club meeting, and I wanted to get there badly. What was stopping me? I didn't want to eat the asparagus. I *had* to eat it to get to the meeting, but I didn't want to. So I was trying to eat it, and at the same time, I was resisting it. "Forget it. I'm not eating this. It's gross." I focused on being repulsed by it. "I can't eat it!" I was fighting against myself. How could I possibly win when I was fighting against *myself*?

Then. Suddenly. I changed my mind. I decided that I *wanted* to eat the asparagus. Why did that work? Because I *had* to eat it to get to the meeting, and I *wanted* to get to the meeting. Once I decided that I wanted to eat it, I stopped fighting with myself and became *totally committed* to the project of eating the (gross) asparagus. I gave my brain one consistent message instead of two conflicting messages, and it instantly came to my rescue, inventing just what I needed to do to eat it.

OK, let me clarify: I didn't *enjoy* eating it. I didn't even *like* eating it. I didn't really even *want* to eat it. If there were another path to get to the meeting, I would have taken it. So what *did* I want? I wanted to do whatever I *had* to do to get where I wanted to go. In this case, the had-to happened to be eating that (slimy) asparagus. By *wanting* to accomplish the task, I quickly figured out a clever way to do it, and the task became easier. I turned the had-to into a want-to.

Think about it. Benjamin's uncle Steve *really* wanted to become a member of the Coast Guard. Jumping out of the helicopter was mandatory to reach his goal. He *had* to accomplish this threatening task to get where he was going. So instead of wasting time fighting with his fear, he invited the scary feelings to come along with him. Why? *Because it was the most efficient way to arrive at his goal.* And he wanted his goal badly. So he turned the had-to into a want-to.

How about Benjamin? He was afraid of going over to his friend Jason's house. He decided he was going to *want* his fear, because if he *didn't* want it, he'd back away from Jason's invitation. It's not that he had to go to Jason's house that day; he could have said no, stayed home and felt more comfortable. But he really wanted to learn to tolerate going over to other kids' houses, and he chose that day to begin practicing. So he welcomed his fear along.

I wanted to go to the neighborhood club meeting. To get there I had to stop fighting with the (grotesque, slimy, disgusting) asparagus. So **I welcomed it into my belly** instead. Uncle Steve got into the Coast Guard, Benjamin enjoyed his time at Jason's house, and I helped build a very cool clubhouse.

How to Enjoy the Movies

This is the move you need to make: if you want to get somewhere—

if you *want* a result—then, please, *want* whatever it takes to get there.

We kids do this all the time and have been doing it all our lives. We want to have some fun (that's the result). And we are willing to do whatever it takes to get that fun. For example: You want to enjoy seeing that new movie with your best friend. There are lots of steps involved in that process.

- You want to leave your house on time.
- You want to ride to the theatre with your friend and get excited about the event together.
- You want to get drinks and popcorn, pick just the right seats, and be there on time to see all the trailers of the new movies. (When the lines are long to get into the theatre, Elliot's been known to slide up front and pretend he's a member of another family.)

Because when it's all over, you want to say to your friend, "That was fun!"

All those things you do—inviting your friend, getting out of the house on time, standing in line for the tickets, finding the right seats—contribute to getting you what you want: fun! Think about this:

- When you *want* to leave the house on time, you do everything you can to accomplish that task. You don't drag your feet.
- When you *want* just the right seats, then you are full of energy to figure out how to get those seats.

You *Can* Get There from Here

If we put on our thinking caps, what do we conclude? See if this seems logical:

1. If you want to get somewhere, then you need to take all the steps that get you there, and

2. If you are also willing to take each of those steps, then the *steps* become easier,

3. And you reach your goal with less trouble.

Does that make sense to you? If you want to go to the movies with your friend, then leaving your house on time is required. If you *want* to leave your house on time, then that step becomes trouble-free. If you want to finish all that ice cream, and you want to taste each delicious spoonful too, then getting to the bottom of the bowl is simple.

But ice cream is easy. And we're not here to do the easy stuff, are we? No. We're here to do the tough stuff. Let's talk.

You say: "OK, maybe I have to do the tough stuff. But why in the world would I want to do the tough stuff?"

I say: "Because that's how you reach your goals. You gotta do the tough stuff to reach your goals."

You: "Yeah, fine. I *have* to do them, but I don't have to *like* it."

Me: "But... if you will change your attitude... if you will experiment with this idea... this is what you will discover: when you truly *want* to do the task that you *have* to do, that task becomes *easier* for you. If you have to do it anyway, why not make it as easy as possible?"

You: "Huh?"

Me: "Let me say it again slowly, because this is a tricky concept: **If you have to do it anyway, then why not make it as easy as possible? Why make a hard job harder**?"

Yes, I know, you are still protesting the idea. This move goes against your current logic, so you'll have to override a longstanding way of looking at things. You're thinking, "Why would anyone *want* an unpleasant experience? That's out-and-out STUPID." But consider that there might be a flaw in your logic.

- Do you want good grades but don't want to study?
- Do you want your allowance but don't want to do your chores?
- Do you want to play in a band but don't want to practice your guitar?
- Do you want to have friends but don't want to ask anyone to go the movies?

You HAVE to take steps to reach your goals. If you stop fighting against each step, you can reach your goals sooner and more easily.

The Best Present Ever

Imagine that at the top of a set of stairs is the birthday present you've wanted all year, just sitting there waiting for you to pick it up. But these are BIG steps. You have to stretch each leg way up and then push with all your might to get to each next step. For some steps, you have to throw your leg up there and then **lay on your belly to pull yourself up**. Do you imagine that when you get to a tough step, you'll just sit down and decide not to go any further? After all, it's hard work. Or would you *want* to take each step, even the hard ones? Would you be *willing to struggle* to make sure you got over the biggest steps? Of course you would, because you want that prize at the top.

But the *added benefit* is that when you WANT to take each step—hard as it may be—you'll focus all your energy and attention on that step. You'll take it as quickly as possible and as efficiently as possible, spending whatever effort you need. You're ready to get *past* that step and on to the next one, because each step gets you closer to the top, where your present awaits.

To achieve anything important, you have to put out effort. Like Erik climbing the seven summits. Effort. That means work. Gathering up your energy and spending it on the project. That's the only way you reach your goals. If you want good grades, you might spend a second or two imagining that report card with all A's. But that's easy, isn't it? It doesn't take a whole lot of energy. To really get what you want, you need to muster up all that wanting and energy and focus it on the *actions* that will get you there. If you want good grades, then the action is to study. Effort. Work.

I really love apple pie, and my Aunt Lisa taught me how to make one. If I have a real craving for pie, it's sooo easy to imagine biting into a forkful of warm pie, with that flakey crust, and the chunks of soft, sweet apple, with a scoop of my favorite vanilla ice cream on top. But if I want to eat some *real* self-made pie (not an imaginary one), I have to focus on the steps… peeling the apples, making the dough, rolling it out, putting it all together. It's worth my time and effort. That's what **gets me a pie, and I want pie**!

When you say, "I don't want to do this but I *have* to," can you see how that message makes it feel harder to get the same amount of stuff done? So, let me repeat: If you want to get somewhere, then you need to take all the steps that get you there. If you also *willingly* take each of those steps, then the *steps* become easier.

Another example: your dad says, "Clean up your room by lunch or no allowance this week." You roll your eyes and shuffle up to your room and stare at the mess. You grumble, "Why do they make me do this? It's *my* room. Why can't I just shut the door?" You take a deep sigh and slowly start picking things up and figuring out where to put them. Then you lay on the bed for a while. When you hear the call of, "lunchtime!" coming from downstairs, you drag yourself out of bed and half-heartedly finish the job, hoping your parents don't notice the dirty clothes you tossed on the closet floor or all the books and papers and trash you shoved under the bed in your final push to get out of the room.

Same example, different approach: your dad says, "Clean up your room by lunch or no allowance this week." You roll your eyes and shuffle up to your bedroom and stare at the mess. You think, "Alright, I gotta get this done. I might as well make the best of it." You turn on some tunes, scan the room, and plan how you'll tackle the mess as you grab the laundry basket from the back of your closet. You make up a little game. "Let me see how few steps I can take while I'm getting this done." As you stand in one place, you grab clothes from the floor around you and toss them in the basket. Then you bend over until you're laying your chest on the bed, scoop up the dirty clothes within reach, lift yourself back up, and toss them in the basket, too. And still you haven't taken a step! **The game goes on, with your favorite music**, until you're done.

And then the call, "Lunchtime!"

Here's my question: in which of these two scenes did you feel better? In which did you accomplish more? One more question: which one did you finish first?

If you *really* want to learn a difficult but interesting subject in school, you need to focus your energy on this: pay attention in class, ask for help when you're confused, and study even when there are other things to do that are more fun. One of the best ways to focus on these three tasks is to say to yourself, "I *want* to pay attention in class" and "I *want* to ask for help, so I'll understand this stuff," and "I *want* to be studying right now." And to really mean it. Yes, of course, part of you will be saying, "I don't want to...." But don't let that voice run the show. It just makes life harder.

Let's imagine you *really* want to play guitar in a band. Really, really. And you know, without question, that you must practice just about every day to reach your goal. When it's time to practice, which of these two messages will help you get around to practicing?

- "I don't want to practice, but I *have* to."
- "I *want* to practice, even though it's hard."

Which thought supports your goal of playing in a band? Which one will help you practice when there are other activities that might be more fun at the moment?

If you apply this want-to attitude to the things you struggle with, then here's what you can get for your efforts:

- When you *want* something, you stop fighting against it, so you will have more energy to get through it.
- When you *want* something, you can better handle the discomfort that might come with it.
- When you *want* something, your brain comes up with creative

ways to get it.

But—hey—don't take my word for it. Try it out. At school, pick some times when you're feeling bored or restless. Each time, decide to spend the next fifteen minutes purposely concentrating on whatever topic the teacher is presenting. Decide that you want to pay attention to the task. Find creative ways to stay alert.

Try this, too. Are there any chores at home that you don't usually like doing? Maybe they're boring or tough for you. *Decide* to make each chore less boring or difficult. Figure out a way to entertain yourself with the chore. (Like maybe you could sing while you're doing it.) Or invent ways to do it more efficiently. (Can you play with emptying all the trash cans in the house with the fewest number of footsteps?) Or create a novel way to complete it. (Perhaps you can vacuum your room in such a way that you leave only a diagonal pattern on the carpet.) Find out what you come up with to challenge yourself.

If you want to try out these experiments, here are three tips:

1. Good reasons motivate us. Have a good reason to "want to." In these situations, the reason can even be "because I want to find out what happens." Be curious.

2. You have to honestly mean it when you think, "I want to..." You can't pretend or just mouth the words. What's the point of that? You're not doing this until you are 50 years old; you're only doing it for a few minutes. Can you spare a few minutes?

3. You have to remind yourself that "I want to do this" about five to ten times during each situation. Otherwise, you'll space out and just do it your usual way.

If you do these experiments, then maybe... just maybe... you'll say something like, "Hey, that was interesting. When I forced myself to want to pay attention in class, time seemed to go by much faster." Or, "when I played around with seeing how few steps I could take while I was emptying all the trash cans, I wasn't as annoyed as I usually am when I do that chore."

In other words, maybe you will begin to see that when you apply the want-to attitude, it helps you **turn not-that-fun stuff into not-so-hard stuff**. Then you'll be ready to think about how it's going to help you do some of the harder stuff.

What's Next?

While I've been teaching you about managing worry, I've told you stories. I want you to remember what you're learning in each chapter, so I told you about Benjamin, Uncle Steve and the Coast Guard, and my trip to the water park, just to name a few. There was the vomit on my dress, of course, and how Bridget freaks out at cross country races. This book wouldn't do you much good if—right after reading the words—you just forget everything I tell you. I want my stories to connect you to new ideas and new ways of responding to worry. If you remember these ideas, then you can try them out for yourself sometime.

Makes sense, right? Pretty obvious, don't you think? Learn something, remember it, use it later. Simple.

I've discovered that worry plays by a different set of rules. It relies on forgetting. Needs it. Waits for it. And you've been falling for it, just like I was. Well, not for long. Keep going and you'll never make a sardine and jellybean pizza again.

Chapter 10: Chutes and Learners

Have you ever played the game called Chutes and Ladders? It's been around forever. Like most board games, you roll the dice and move your piece along the board, racing to the finish. When you land on the bottom of a ladder, you're allowed to skip lots of spaces by climbing the ladder toward the finish. (I love that part.) When you land on the top of a chute—it looks like a big playground slide—you zoom back down, losing most of the progress you've made. (I don't love that part so much.)

I can honestly say I'm *not* a big fan of starting over. I once accidentally used salt instead of sugar when I was making cookies, and I had to throw the entire batter out and begin again. My mom was painting the bathroom a few months ago, and realized halfway through that she hated the color, so she chose to start over with a different shade of blue. Annoying.

I could make a very long list of the times when I had to start over. You could, too, I'm sure. Because unless you're perfect, you're going to screw up, or forget something, or open a can of cat food when you meant to open a can of tuna. (Yeah, I did that, too.) Some people build their entire careers on starting over, on purpose. People who do medical research, design new cars or toys, create recipes, write books, draw comics. Back to the drawing board, they say. Where do you think that expression came from, anyway?

Now here's something you might not know: there are two different ways of "starting over." Because this is a book about managing worry, you can probably guess that one way of starting over is helpful as you move through your day. The other way? Well, let's just say it would not be endorsed by the **Casey Council of Effective Worry Management**. And the difference between the two? It's whether you *remember* or *forget* what you've already learned.

Examples? You want examples? I was just getting to that. Here are two.

Imagine what school would be like if you forgot the alphabet every night after dinner and had to start back at "A" each day. You'd never get past letter H, I'm guessing. Or imagine a chef who is hoping to discover an amazing new combination of pizza toppings. After putting jellybeans and sardines together, he sadly concludes that it is totally vile. The next day he forgets what he has already tried, and says to himself, "I've got an idea. **How about sardines and jellybeans this time**?"

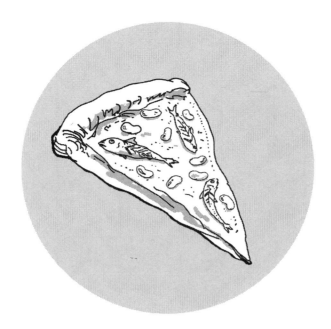

When worry shows up, it often makes your forget what you've learned before, like how you handled a fire drill, or a visit to the doctor, or the first day of school last year. You're trying to do new things, and step forward. But with worry in charge, it feels like you're starting over *completely*, right back to letter A.

When worry is *not* the boss, you still have to start over at times— we all do!—but you start over with what you've learned along the way. You talk to yourself about the things you do well, or the times when you handled your fear or worried thoughts. You make changes based on what you discover (I learned to put labels on the sugar and the salt containers, by the way) and your memory of all of those events starts to add up to something helpful: experience.

Erik Weihenmayer learned how to rock-climb, using ropes to keep him safe. Climbing El Capitan in Yosemite National Park was incredibly difficult, but he used all the skills he remembered from previous, easier climbs, to accomplish this feat. Then he used all his rock-climbing skills to ice-climb up the Losar waterfall in the Himalaya Mountains. That's what everybody needs to do: remember skills we've already learned and apply them to our new adventures.

I had to learn this. I'm sure that comes as no surprise. When I started fourth grade, I was having a hard time adjusting and I didn't know how to talk to myself. That was five years ago but I can still remember it like it was yesterday. I felt like I was starting over every night when I sat down to do my homework. My worry was giving Mom and me all sorts of trouble. We figured it out, but it took a while. See if any of my story sounds familiar.

The Reminder Bridge

My fourth grade teacher, Mrs. O'Shea, smiled almost all the time.

She didn't yell, but we all listened to her. Everyone liked Mrs. O'Shea. Fourth grade, she told us on the second day of school, would be a bit different. We were older, and it was time for more homework and more responsibility. It was time for tests and quizzes, and some writing projects that we would do at home. Looking back, I think my worry about homework started right then and there. "I can't do that! I've never done that before! How will I know what to do?" My worries had my full attention, so I didn't listen to what she said next. I heard it, but I didn't listen: "You don't know how to do these things yet. We're here to learn together and build up our skills, step by step. Be ready to learn new things, and be ready for the mistakes that will certainly happen along the way!" Of course, she was smiling. Of course, I didn't pay any attention.

My worries told me that I had to get everything *right*. Mrs. O'Shea gave us homework, as promised, and I sat at the kitchen table, sometimes for hours, **making sure every letter was perfect**. I checked my math problems over and over to make sure they were right, and if I didn't understand something, I cried and I yelled at Mom.

Mom didn't let this go on for very long. She called Mrs. O'Shea, who reassured her that I was doing great. She told Mom, and then told me in school, that she expected mistakes from all her students (including me). "You're just starting to learn how to study and write reports and take tests." I noticed other kids at school making mistakes, and some couldn't finish all their homework. I saw Mrs. O'Shea's smiling face, and I heard her kind words of encouragement. I did make mistakes at school, and Mrs. O'Shea happily helped me to correct them. I was learning fourth grade math, step by step, right on schedule. I took tests and did well on many of them. When I did poorly, no one yelled or punished me.

But at night, away from Mrs. O'Shea, the worries grabbed my attention again. They convinced me I had to be perfect or I'd get in trouble and that I wouldn't be able to learn how to do fourth grade work. The worried thoughts made me feel frustrated, and I often cried and ripped up my papers.

One night as I sat at the table, **I began crying and threw my pencil**. When Mom told me to put away my homework and go to my room (she finally had enough of my nightly tantrums), I yelled at her and told her I was stupid. I told her I *couldn't* learn NO MATTER WHAT!

Mom walked over to my backpack and not-so-calmly pulled the zipper open. She removed my take-home folder and put two pieces of paper down in front of me. One was a spelling test. I had gotten three wrong but had corrected them with Mrs. O'Shea's help. Across the top of the paper, in red letters, Mrs. O'Shea wrote "BETTER EVERY TIME!" and drew a smiling face. The other paper was math homework. I had every question correct on that one. There was a star next to my name.

"I have told you over and over," my mother reassured me, "that you are learning what you need to learn and that mistakes are part of learning. I know you've heard me say, 'Being perfect is impossible.' You're a great student. You keep FORGETTING this every time you sit down and take out your homework. How are you going to make it stick?"

I didn't know the answer to that question and that made it a rough night. I kept saying that I *couldn't* handle fourth grade, even though I was managing it just fine. How could I make all those encouraging words and reassurances stick in my mind? What was I doing wrong? I didn't know then, but I do now.

My worries were so strong at homework time—and I believed them so completely—that I was FORGETTING what I had accomplished during the day and what I heard from Mom and Mrs. O'Shea. It was as if all the things I knew about me as a fourth grader disappeared as soon as worry showed up. Down the chute I would go. When you're worrying and feeling anxious, it's pretty easy to forget all the successes you've had.

Actually, that was a rough year all around. Even though Mom and Mrs. O'Shea both tried to reassure me, I worried a lot about being stupid. I was really hard on myself and spent *far* too much time on my school projects. Nothing changed until fourth grade was over and Mom and Elliot and I headed off to the beach for a week of fun in the sun. As we were driving, and while Elliot was sleeping in the back seat, all my upsets started spilling out again.

"I don't want to go through this next year! Why do I have to **wait 'til summer to have fun**? That's only two months out of twelve. It's not fair!"

Somehow, Mom must have thought I was ready to learn something new. She was also probably ready to drop me off on the side of the road. "I'll tell you what I do. Maybe it can help you. As you know, I do tend to worry a lot." I rolled my eyes. "But I try not to let it last too long. When I catch myself worrying, I look for ways to build a bridge." For a moment, I thought she was talking about a real bridge, like the one we were going to cross to get to the beach. But, no.

"**I imagine a bridge** that connects whatever I have to do now with something similar in my past. I look for a time when I succeeded, when I handled a similar problem well. I call it my reminder bridge.

"I started doing this when you were a little baby, because as a new mom I worried about doing everything right. I had done a lot of babysitting before I had you, so I would imagine a reminder bridge connecting what I knew as a babysitter to what I could do as a mom. I didn't have to start over learning about babies."

She said it was even easier when my brother was born. She just made a bridge between being a mom to me and being a mom to Elliot. She had worries, but she didn't let them get in the way of that connection.

136

Cool, huh? And it brings us to the next piece of the puzzle. I know the word "bridge" is usually a noun, but let's make it a verb: BRIDGE BACK TO YOUR SUCCESSES.

That one conversation got my mind moving in a new direction. By the end of beach week, I started to understand what I was missing. My worries were keeping me from the thoughts and memories that could comfort me and give me confidence. I sure could have used that kind of reminder bridge when I was in fourth grade, sitting down to do my homework. If I had been able to remember all of the good work I was doing at school, and all the positive words about my successes I was hearing from Mrs. O'Shea and Mom, I might have skipped all that stress and worry! By talking to myself in a different way, I would have connected with all the things I knew already.

Santa Claus Eats an Ice Cream

My friend Lindsay (who is not afraid of roller coasters, as you may recall) is dreadfully afraid of bees. She does *not* want to get stung. When she sees a bee buzzing around the blossoms on a bush, she thinks to herself, "I'm afraid of bees. I hope I don't get stung." I'd say that's a pretty normal thought to have about bees. They have stingers, and it really hurts when you get stung. But then Lindsay *keeps thinking* about getting stung. She even imagines a whole swarm of bees chasing her. She thinks about trying to run and tripping while they chase her. All of this thinking happens very fast, so when she sees a bee, she runs away and screams a lot. Last spring and summer, she just plain refused to come outside and play. "I don't want to see any bees," she'd say. "They terrify me."

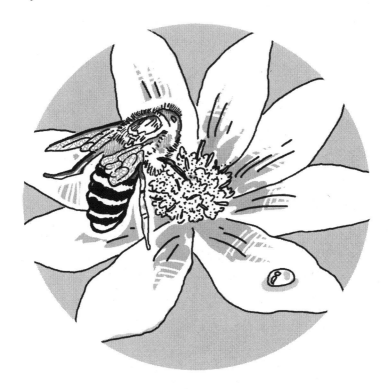

When you get stuck in worry, the worried thought moves in, unpacks its bags and stays. And stays. A worried thought, to really succeed at being an effective worried thought—to win the blue ribbon at the **Annual Worried Thoughts Achievement Dinner**—has to stick around. It has to stick around long enough to get you to do these things:

STOP

BACK AWAY

In Chapter 1 you learned about these benefits of worry—to stop and back away. Sometimes stopping is great because it gives you a chance to figure out what to do next. But when you get *stuck* in a worry, you aren't flexible like the cooked spaghetti. You're not saying, "Hey, let me stop for a minute and discuss my different choices." No. A stuck worry tells you to STOP whenever you feel afraid or uncomfortable. It says, "Wait! I can't handle this! Freeze! No moving forward!" A stuck worry creates **dig-in-your-heels, cross-your-arms, don't-even-talk-about-it** stopping. My aunt calls it "putting down all fours," like a stubborn mule does when you're trying to pull it out of its stall. I think you might know what she means.

Sometimes avoiding is also a good choice, like avoiding a beehive or a very busy traffic intersection on your bike. But when you get stuck in a worry, you BACK AWAY, because that's the quickest way to feel comfortable again. You say to yourself, "Don't even try it! You'll feel bad, and you hate that feeling. Stay where it's safe and comfortable." When worry gets stuck inside you, it creates BIG avoiding. You say, "I know loud noises scare me, and there might be loud noises at birthday parties, so I'm going to avoid all birthday parties."

There's a third thing that stuck worry does, and I'll bet you don't know this one. Getting stuck in worry makes you FORGET. You forget all the experiences in your life when you *did* try something new and it worked out, or when you were learning good things even though you made mistakes. You can't remember the times when you handled uncomfortable feelings, and still made it through okay. You don't recall how you felt shy at first when the new babysitter came over, until she gave you chocolate milk and showed you **how to make water balloons**.

Stuck worries do just that—get you stuck. Here's how it adds up:
STOP + BACK AWAY + FORGET = STUCK

So... how do you get unstuck? If worried thoughts bother you, why don't you just quit having those thoughts? Can you do that? Let's do an experiment. Take a deep breath. Blink your eyes three times. Now, don't... no matter what...*don't*, under any circumstances, imagine...a... **GIANT PURPLE OCTOPUS**.

Well? Do you remember what not to imagine?

There! You imagined one, didn't you? Everyone else reading this book did, too. Kids and grown-ups. *I'm* even imagining a giant purple octopus right now.

I told you *not* to think of something, and you thought of it anyway. Why? Because our brains work that way. They are very busy places full of thoughts and images. The things we think about might come from what we hear or see, what someone tells us, or a memory that comes to mind for some reason. Once we think about something, it's practically impossible to *not* think about it again by telling ourselves *not* to think about it. You can try it a few more times if you need more proof.

Don't imagine **Santa Claus eating an ice cream cone**.

Now here's a tough one: *don't hear* the sound of a siren on a **fire truck**. The sound that's coming up upon you, getting **louder and louder**, but you don't see it yet, and you aren't sure what direction it's coming from.

See what I mean? Maybe someone has instructed to you, "Now, don't worry about that, honey." Or perhaps, if you're trying not to get spooked at bedtime, you say to yourself, "I'm *not* going to think about the monster in the closet. I'm *not* going to think about the monster in the closet." You say it over and over again, and your image of the monster in the closet gets clearer and bigger. You were only trying to feel better, and now you feel worse.

If you could stop worrying by just not thinking, then the plan would be this:

STOP THINKING. STOP WORRYING.

That's it. No need to write a book. I could make bumper stickers, or hire one of **those airplanes that pull big banners** behind it to fly around the country. Simple.

But we can't stop thinking. None of us can. Maybe for a second or two here and there, but even when we sleep, our brains are busy with this and that. If we know we can't stop thinking, then what do we do? I gave some pretty convincing reasons in Chapter 4 that our first response should be, "it's okay the worry popped up." Remember some of the reasons? Worry shows up because sometimes it's helpful to slow down or back away. Plus, sometimes our great imaginations can scare us. What else can influence how much we worry? How our parents act around us, our genetic makeup, and our need to do everything perfectly.

Then there are all those times that worry tends to show up:

- you're doing something new or different
- you're unsure about your plans
- you have a lot of "what if" questions
- you have to perform
- something scary is happening

So your first response is, "it's okay that the worry popped up." What's the next response? "I can let this worry go," or "I can handle this." Some worries are going to be dumb or at least not helpful, like "If the Earth stops turning on its axis one night when I'm sleeping, it'll be DARK FOREVER!" You can practice dropping them when you hear them, or talking to your worry, like I explained in Chapter 5. ("You're just feeling scared. Everything's going to be okay.")

Taking the Sting Out

For some other worries, reminding yourself how you've handled a fear—remembering what you've done and can do again—is very helpful. I'll show you what I mean. Now, I'm not perfect, by any stretch of the imagination. But handling bees is one thing I do well. Like Lindsay, I'm not a huge fan of bees either. I was stung when I was three, and I stepped on one when I was eleven. It hurt, but I survived. When I see a bee, I have the same thought as Lindsay. The same exact thought. "I'm afraid of bees. I hope I don't get stung." But here's the difference: I just have the thought (even though it's not a very pleasant thought), and I move on. I really do hope I don't get stung, but I know I can handle it if it happens. And I figured out a while ago that if I pay attention to where the bees are, I'm pretty good at avoiding them. Since I have a plan that works (that's just plain smart, if you ask me), then that worry is just a momentary thought. It can be there, and I can hear it, but it is not breaking news, and it doesn't set off any alarms inside me.

In Chapter 3 I talked about how we can sometimes imagine bad things happening on a plane. Well, I asked just about every grownup I know if, when they fly, they think about the plane crashing. Do you know what they said? Of course they do—but only for a moment. The flight attendants talk about problems at the start of every flight. They point out the emergency exits and the oxygen masks. They show you how to put on your life vest. **You can't help but think about it!**

Those people—the ones who fly with only a little worry—will think that thought, know it's normal, and then move on. They're not surprised to feel a tad worried. Who wouldn't feel worried for a moment? But they already know that they don't need to address the worry, so they let it go. Same now with me: if I think it's not helpful to dwell on my worries, I know how to let them go.

- Every time I see a bee, I have my bee thoughts—for a moment. Then I automatically bridge to my successes with handling bees in the past. I know I can do it again.
- Every time I get on a plane, I have my crashing thoughts—for a moment. I automatically bridge to my past, when I decided that I **don't need to worry** about that topic.
- On the first day of school, I usually have my uneasy new-school-year thoughts. I automatically bridge to my memories of handling the first-day jitters in past years.
- When I go to the dentist, I worry a bit about new cavities. For a moment. I automatically bridge to how I handled the two fillings I've had in the past.

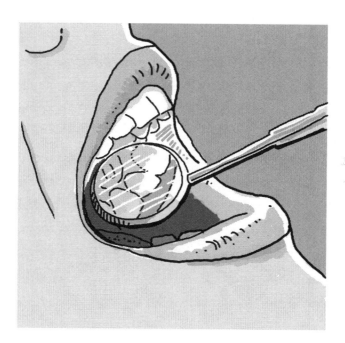

I'll bet you noticed that I keep saying I "automatically" bridge. I promise you that I did not "automatically" do anything on this list when I started out. When I was eleven, after stepping on that bee and getting stung, I got scared just like Lindsay, and I worried about getting stung again. I hesitated about going outside most of that spring. But I wanted to play outside more than I wanted to never again be stung. So every day when I ventured outside, I'd check out where the bees were, and I'd carefully watch for them. Pretty much every day I had to remember that a sting really hurts for a second or two, then hurts some (stings, really) for twenty more minutes or so, and then I forget about it.

Over and over I had to repeat that pattern: remind myself that I wanted to go outside badly enough to overcome my fear. Check around for bees. And remember how I can handle it on the rare occasion that I do get stung. Every day. Most of that spring. And by summer, it was a routine pattern: **worry for a moment**, bridge *automatically* to my successes, and **move on**.

You can do this, too. Really, you can. You can hear those worried thoughts pop up, and then you can just let them go and move forward into your next activity. In the beginning, you'll need help letting those worries go, just as I did. Just as everybody does. That's what this book is for.

Now, as a ninth grader, I've built a bridge that connects me back to lots of the things I have learned and the good work I have done. Even when I feel overwhelmed, I now remember that I'm a good learner. The reminder bridge is right there when I need it. I still get frustrated, but I don't forget for long that I am a good student and that I've learned tons of things since kindergarten.

These are the kind of things I say to myself:

Some of Casey's Reminder Bridges

I've done fine in all the other grades, so I'll probably be able to handle this grade, too.

My teachers have taught me that mistakes are part of learning.

I usually feel worried when I'm starting something, but I get the hang of it quickly.

I haven't learned this *exact* thing yet, but I have a lot of experience learning new things.

Every time I have to start over, I have something to build on from the last time.

I know the idea of talking to yourself sounds funny, but all kids and grownups do it all through their days. As you construct your own bridge, you'll say things that are helpful for *your* situation. The details will be different. Maybe for you, it's being able to go away to camp or handle the big dog at your new friend's house. No matter what the situation, talking to yourself in this way usually sounds something like this:

Examples of Bridging to Success

I really want to...	*That reminds me of how...*	*That reminds me how I can handle...*
go to that summer camp for a week	I started sleeping over at Seth's house	being uncomfortable at first
jump off the high diving board	I learned last summer to dive off the edge of the pool	feeling scared the first time I try it
try out for the school musical	I got cut from the soccer team the first year, but made it the next year	not knowing if I'll make it, and even getting cut, too, if that happens
raise my hand and answer questions in class	I answered everybody's questions about my project at the science fair	feeling nervous and doing it anyway

Get the hang of it? When you talk like this, you're helping yourself come to two important conclusions:

1. I have experience with this kind of thing.

2. I think I can handle it.

When you try something new and use skills from your past successes, will it always turn out exactly as you want it to? No.

Will it be uncomfortable? Maybe.

Will it be hard? Could be.

Do you really want it? That's the big question to answer. It's going to help lots if you really want to reach this goal.

Here are all the pieces of the puzzle. (I wrote it up and posted it on the refrigerator. For three weeks I read it almost every time I got something to eat or drink.) We're going to talk more about that "step on into that new situation" one in the next chapter. It represents our last piece: TAKE ACTION ON YOUR PLAN.

Casey's Really Clever Guide to Winning over Worries

Know what you want to accomplish.
Remember your past successes that can help you.
Expect worry to show up.
Talk to your worries so they can't run the show.
And step on into that new situation.
Be willing to feel unsure
& uncomfortable along the way.
Let your breathing skills support you.

What's Next

This past January I started working on the back stage crew for our school musical. Painting scenery, finding props, stuff like that. While my backstage crew pals and I were moving down our list of projects, the actors (including my friend Shannon) were learning their lines and songs and dance steps. During the first month, we hardly saw each other.

About a week before the show, we finally had all the sets painted, costumes ready, and props together. The backstage crew and the actors met at the stage for the regular Thursday night rehearsal, and we started putting it all together. The scenes looked amazing (except for the door that kept falling off the hinges, so we fixed that). The actors loved **dueling with the swords** we made for them instead of just pretending. The characters came alive wearing the costumes we made. (We did have to make a few adjustments, of course. But that's what rehearsals are for: to get the kinks out. Like Wallace Culvert's pants. The first pair was so short, Shannon said they looked more like capris, and Wallace wasn't having any of that.)

The show was a big hit. Our parents loved it. (Please! Of course, they did.) I was exhausted and excited at the same time. I loved watching it go from nothing but a bunch a kids meeting in the cafeteria, to a razzle-dazzle, sword-fighting, toe-tapping production.

Right now, I'm feeling the same way. I've spent these last ten chapters helping you understand all the parts we need to manage worry, and what it takes to move forward into new experiences. And we've even been doing a bit of rehearsing in our minds, haven't we?

So let's see what it looks like when we start **putting it all together**. Elliot, my favorite guinea pig, is going to help. He came up against a challenge, and we came up with a plan.

Chapter 11: Answering the Bell

Elliot usually bounded in from school like a big-pawed young tiger and asked Mom for a snack, without any moaning. But one day a few weeks after he started school this year, he shuffled through the front door, dropped his backpack on the kitchen floor, crossed his arms over his chest, and announced he was not going back to school. Mom tilted her head, wrinkled her brow, and didn't say anything. Just kind of stared. We both knew that Elliot liked his teacher, and his best friend Teddy was in the same class.

A Hasty Retreat

"We had a fire drill today," Elliot finally blurted out. "The principal told the whole school we would have more of them during the year, so **I'm not going back**."

"Elliot, all schools have them. It's not a big deal," I said. He shot me a dirty look, then turned back to Mom.

"The noise was so loud when it went off! I jumped in my chair. My heart was pounding. The teachers were talking loud too, and not being friendly. I didn't like it at all. I don't want to do any more of those!" His eyes filled with tears.

(By the way, I think if I had come home and made this

announcement in first grade, Mom would have called the school to find out all the fire drill days. And she would have kept me home. I would have liked it at the time, but I understand now how that doesn't really help kids with their worries. Elliot was lucky that afternoon, because Mom had already started learning about worry with me. She knew what to say and do with him.)

Mom pulled Elliot onto her lap. "Fire alarms *are* loud. I used to jump every time they went off in my school, and sometimes they go off at work. They're designed to be loud, so we all pay attention and move out of the building right away. If fire alarms were soft little chimes, we'd probably ignore them, or take our time dawdling along. It sounds like your body did just what it was supposed to do."

Elliot just stared at the floor, and Mom continued, "So the loud alarm scared you, and your body did just what it's supposed to do when it gets startled by a loud noise. Now, you're worried about having that same feeling in your body again, aren't you?"

He nodded. (Boy, Mom was good at this stuff!) "But, Mom…." It sounded like he was pleading at this point. "I don't like the way it sounds when it's so loud, and I don't like feeling that scared."

"Who does!" Mom said, more as a statement than a question. "So let's figure out what to do. We know fire drills will happen. We don't know exactly when. And we know you won't like them much. What do we do?"

"Stay home from school!" Elliot yelled, laughing and crying at the same time.

"Well, that's one way to deal with it," Mom agreed. "But I'd rather you learn to handle loud noises rather than try to stay away from all of them. Loud noises happen. We can't get rid of them. We probably can't even stop being startled by them. It's a natural response. Dogs, cats, mice, birds, even **elephants, are startled by loud noises**." Then Mom looked my way and nodded her head. That was my cue.

"Here's what I'd do, Elliot," I said helpfully. If the truth be told, I wasn't just being generous. I had my own motive for helping Elliot. Mom and I were looking for another guinea pig to try out our Plan. Together we made a worksheet that moved through the steps and reminded us to ask some important questions. We used it on me six times already. And with my cousin Joey when he was afraid to take the bus to school. We even helped Mom after she hit that deer and then didn't want to drive at night anymore. Mom had made a bunch of clean copies, and I wanted to use one with Elliot. "I'd **have a plan for the next fire drill**. And I mean an *inside* plan. What you're going to say and do inside you. You need to know what to say to worry, what to do with your worried thoughts. And you can practice it in your imagination. Do you want to see if we can come up with a good plan?"

His head barely moved north and south. I took that as a "yes." He didn't really want to quit school. He just didn't know what else to do. I ran off to get a worksheet before he changed his mind. Big sister to the rescue!

How Not to Be Alarmed

Then I started asking him the problem solving questions that Mom and I had worked out.

Me: First thing you have to decide is: what do you want?

Elliot: I want them to stop doing fire drills!

Me: Yes, yes, I know. And I want to get all A's without studying so much. But these are things we can't change. The schools are going to keep setting off those alarms every once in a while. You said you wanted to stop going to school. Is that really what you want?

Elliot: No—I want to be with my friends in class. I'd be bored sitting around home all day.

Me: OK, that's it. [I wrote on our form "Stay in school with my friends."] Do you really want to be able to stay in school?

Elliot: [He looked right at me.] Yes. [Then he looked down at his shoes.] But I'm scared of the alarm!

Me: [checking off that box] I know. We'll get to that. One step at a time. If you want to handle your scare, you have to have something important that you're shooting for. Wanting to hang out with your friends at school will motivate you. [On to the next topic.] Do you remember our camping weekend this summer in the mountains? [He nodded.] What interesting thing happened?

Elliot: [tilting his head and wrinkling his brow for a moment, then smiling] Oh! The snake! That was fun!

Now he says it was fun. But as we were hiking down a road in the State Park, we walked right up to a big black snake, probably four feet long. Mom was in the lead, and she first thought it was a stick. Then, when it moved, she **let out a big scream and jumped back**. Then I screamed. Then Elliot screamed. He didn't see the snake yet, but our screaming made him think it'd be worth it to go ahead and scream, too. Finally he saw the snake, jumped back, and screamed again. We were all afraid, for about eight seconds. Then we slowly got closer. And leaned over. Our scare turned to excitement and curiosity as we watched it gracefully slide across the dirt, stop for a few moments, and move again, until it disappeared into the grass. But not before Elliot got to take a picture. On the second day of school he brought the photo in for show-and-tell—the snake, my feet, and Mom's feet. It was cool.

Me: When you saw the snake, did you feel different than when you hear that fire alarm?

Elliot: No. I jumped, and even yelled, and I could feel my heart beating hard.

Me: Then what?

Elliot: Well, Mom said it was a safe snake and started stepping closer to it, so I did too. It was really cool. And I got to take a picture of it.

We talked for a while about how quickly he got over being scared that day, and how he could do it again when he heard the alarm. He could even decide to look around at the other kids to see how they were reacting. That would give him a new project, just like studying the snake.

Next, I helped him bridge from the snake event to the alarm event. I started by asking him what he thinks after being startled by the alarm.

Elliot: I think, "I can't stand this. Make it stop!"

Me: If you could remember what you did with the snake, what would you say to yourself?

Elliot: I'd say, "This won't last very long. I can handle this. Let me think about something else now."

Me: Excellent! I'll write that down. I've got one more question: if it probably won't last very long, are you willing to be scared by the alarm?

Elliot: I don't know... [I just waited a few moments when he said that.] I guess so. [It wasn't a vigorous agreement, but I'd take it.]

Me: Great! Want me to show you a way to start calming down after that alarm goes off?

He gave a little nod. He was looking like a combination of "I really want this to work" and "I don't know if I can do this." It made his face twist up in a funny way, but I kept myself from laughing.

At this point I taught him how to take a Calming Breath. (Remember? From Chapter 8.) Then I was ready to finish off the Plan.

> *Me*: So, here's how it goes. You're sitting in class, minding your own business. Suddenly you hear that loud alarm, and instantly jump. Your heart is racing, just like with the snake. Now what do you do?
>
> *Elliot*: I tell myself, "This won't last very long. I can handle it." And then I look around to see what the other kids are doing. Like a detective, right?
>
> *Me*: Right. And if you want help calming down?
>
> *Elliot*: I take one of those breaths.
>
> *Me*: You got it!

I helped Elliot imagine all the steps. We ran through it three times, until he rolled his eyes and asked, "Can we stop now?" I thought that was a good sign: he was imagining how he would handle being scared, and he was getting bored doing it.

After we finished creating the plan, Elliot seemed to relax his face a little bit, like he felt some relief because he had a plan of action. (That was my goal.) I'm sure he still didn't like fire drills and he still worried some about them, mainly because he didn't know when they would happen. His plan, though, reminded him that his body's reactions were normal, and it included how to manage that first moment of surprise. He now thought, "The fire alarm will make me uncomfortable, but I'll be able to handle it." That's probably why he looked a <u>little</u> more relaxed.

Then came the fun part (for me, at least). We showed our plan (written on our worksheet) to Mom.

The Game Plan

What is your goal?
Handle the fire alarm so I can be with my friends in class.

Do you really want this goal?
   ☐ No, it's not important to me
   ☑ Yes. I want it, but I'm not sure I can get there.

What skills do you need to reach your goal?
1) be willing to be startled 2) wait it out 'til I start feeling better & take a Calming Breath
3) talk to myself when I'm worried 4) use my courage

What do you already know how to do that might help you reach this goal?
Got startled by the snake, but waited it out & got curious. Even took picture.

What do you want to say to yourself when you start to worry?
"This won't last long. I can handle it. Let me think about something else now."

Are you willing to not know exactly how things will turn out?
   ☐ No! I HAVE to know, or I don't want to do it!
   ☑ Yes. I might not like it, but I'll use my courage.

Are you willing to feel physically uncomfortable along the way?
   ☐ No! I HAVE to be calm or I won't do it!
   ☑ Yes. I might not like it, but I'll use my courage.

What can you do to practice your skills?
Let Casey startle me with pot-banging. Win prizes!

The three of us agreed that Elliot needed a little practice. Here's what we came up with:

1. For the next five days, Mom allowed me to sneak up on Elliot (but stay at least ten feet away from him) and suddenly beat on a pot with a mixing spoon.

2. Elliot would jump (he didn't have to work at that; it came automatically.)

3. He'd then say out loud, "This won't last long. I can handle it." (At school he'll say it in his mind. Out loud was just for practice.)

4. Then he'd take a Calming Breath and let himself settle back down.

5. Each of the five times that he talks to himself and takes a Calming Breath (and doesn't yell at me for scaring him), Mom gives him a prize.

He did great. He only yelled at me the second time. That's because I was standing ten feet *above* him on the stairs as he came by. So he earned four prizes, in this order: a pack of gum, a silver dollar, pizza out with a friend, and a two-foot long stuffed snake. (He named him Alfonz the Adder).

Several weeks went by. One morning at breakfast, Elliot announced, "I've been thinking about the fire drill noise. It's going to happen soon." (His school held them about once a month.)

"And?" Mom asked.

"I'm ready to test out my plan. I know I'll jump, then feel my heart beat, but I've been reminding myself that I can handle it," he explained with a voice that was more steady than I expected. "I might be uncomfortable, but then I'll be okay. I hear my worried thoughts, but I'm not putting them in charge."

I was pretty impressed, I have to admit. He'd already reduced our plan down to a manageable three points: I'll get startled, I can handle that, and I don't need my worries to scare me *more*. Elliot was ready to handle his worries in a different way.

After the next fire drill, he came home from school with a different story to tell. "I didn't like it," he explained. "I was a little worried in the morning before it went off. It was loud, and it surprised me, and I jumped! Just another annoying fire drill, I guess. But I did okay."

Elliot's success persuaded me to put the next piece of the puzzle together: TAKE ACTION ON YOUR PLAN.

TAKE ACTION
on your plan

Now, of course, we kids have different worries about different things. Lindsay might be nervous about bees, and Bridget about running races, and Elliot about fire drills, and… you get the idea. But this is what I want you to understand: the way worry operates is pretty consistent. You don't have to start over with every new worry, every unfamiliar situation. Once you learn how your worry works, you can use this plan. Sure, make a few adjustments. Like adding chocolate chips to your favorite oatmeal cookie recipe, or putting on an extra layer of clothes on a chillier day of sledding. The core of the plan stays the same.

Let me show you exactly what I'm talking about.

What's Next

I have confession to make. At the end of Chapter 10, when I was describing how we "put it all together" for the school play, I made it sound like Shannon and I just showed up, took on our jobs, zoomed through rehearsals, and enjoyed the performances. Perhaps (okay, definitely) it wasn't quite that simple. Neither Shannon nor I had ever done a musical at school before. We really *wanted* to try it, but we were nervous…

Hello, plan. Hello, musical. Hello, fun.

Hello, next chapter.

Chapter 12: The Show Must Go On!

On a Monday morning this past January, Shannon and I were sitting in homeroom, listening to Assistant Principal Campbell's voice coming over the speakers with the daily announcements.

"Anyone interested in participating in the musical this year should come to the cafeteria after school on Wednesday for an informational meeting. Everyone's welcome."

We looked at each other. I think Shannon raised her eyebrows at me, so I raised mine back at her. "Maybe?" we seemed to be saying to each other. At lunch we talked about doing it. Shannon was in chorus, and everyone knew she had a good voice. I couldn't sing at all, but I figured there were other jobs for me backstage.

"We should at least go to the meeting and see what we think," I said. Shannon agreed. But that was Monday. At lunch.

By the time we got home from school, hanging out in my kitchen eating potato chips, we were feeling a bit uncertain. I don't remember who spoke first, but it didn't take long before we sounded like this:

"I'm not sure about this. I mean, I've never done this before."

"Yeah, and who knows how much time it will take. I think they rehearse a lot."

"What if kids make fun of me on stage? Can you imagine just **forgetting what you're supposed to do, in front of everybody**?"

"My mom will be less than happy if I can't get my homework done. I'm not sure about this."

Mom came up from the basement at that moment. "Not sure about what?"

We told her we were thinking about doing the musical, but then launched into our list of doubts and worries. She didn't let us get too far.

"Casey! What a perfect opportunity. A new situation, some doubt and discomfort. A whole lot of what if-ing..."

My face suddenly brightened up. "Of course!" Shannon's eyes kept shifting between Mom and me. She looked even more nervous now that I seemed to abandon the resistance.

Yes, time to *work the game plan*. And this time, we had two guinea pigs for the price of one. To the refrigerator door I went, where I removed this laminated masterpiece and then slapped it on the table. Look familiar?

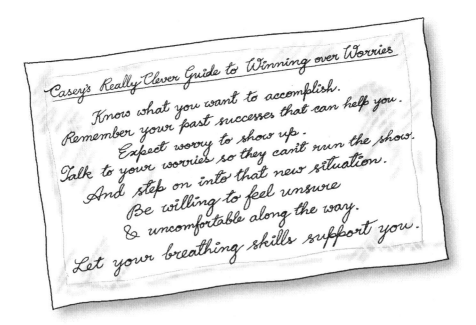

Casey's Really Clever Guide to Winning over Worries

Know what you want to accomplish.
Remember your past successes that can help you.
Expect worry to show up.
Talk to your worries so they can't run the show.
And step on into that new situation.
Be willing to feel unsure
& uncomfortable along the way.
Let your breathing skills support you.

We learned a lot from Elliot's fire drill experiment, so I went up to his room and looked for the piece of paper with our questions and answers on it. (It was under his bed. The cat was sleeping on it.) As I smoothed it out on the table with both hands, I said to Shannon (who had shifted to a silent, wide-eyed look for the last few minutes), "We're going to do the musical. It's necessary. And it's for the good of scientific research. I'll help." Shannon glanced over the two pieces of paper in front of her—my Guide and Elliot's Game Plan—and agreed. I think she just decided to trust me as her coach. Sort of.

Mom went to the computer and printed out some fresh, clean copies of the forms. We got right to work on them. (I must say that it really does get easier with practice.) This was all new to Shannon, so we started with mine. We took it a step at a time, with some explaining along the way. Mom helped, as usual.

The Game Plan

What is your goal?

Do you really want this goal?
- ☐ No, it's not important to me
- ☐ Yes. I want it, but I'm not sure I can get there.

What skills do you need to reach your goal?

What do you already know how to do that might help you reach this goal?

What do you want to say to yourself when you start to worry?

Are you willing to not know exactly how things will turn out?
- ☐ No! I HAVE to know, or I don't want to do it!
- ☐ Yes. I might not like it, but I'll use my courage.

Are you willing to feel physically uncomfortable along the way?
- ☐ No! I HAVE to be calm or I won't do it!
- ☐ Yes. I might not like it, but I'll use my courage.

What can you do to practice your skills?

Here's how it went:

Me: So, first I need to have a goal. I have to know what I want. My goal is to be a part of the musical, because I've never tried it before, but everyone I talk to about it says it's a blast. I can't sing, but I'll bet there are plenty of jobs I can do, and I'll probably make some new friends. And am I sure I want this goal? Yes, I am. My worry may try to say otherwise, but I'm sure. [I was writing quickly as I spoke. Shannon was reading over my shoulder.]

Shannon: So this next part...what skills do you need to reach your goal? What does that mean?

Me: Well, there are skills we use to deal with worry, especially when we're doing something new. Here. Look at this list. [I pulled the laminated list in front of us.] We're going to expect to feel uncomfortable and to have a lot of questions at first, but we're going to know when the worry is trying to get in our way, and we're going to talk back to it. "Look, worry, I really want this, and feeling uncomfortable is normal. You may be telling me to quit, but **I'm not going to listen to you** right now." Like that. Get it? And then maybe take some Calming Breaths, which tells the alarm system to stand down. And then, I'm going to look forward to feeling uncomfortable. I'm going to wait for it. Because I know that when I feel uncomfortable, it means I'm doing something new, something unfamiliar, and I'm giving myself an opportunity to grow and have fun. I'm stepping into a new experience instead of away from it, and that's my goal.

Shannon: So we're supposed to feel uncomfortable? Why would I want to feel uncomfortable?

Mom: It sounds strange at first, doesn't it? But we've figured out that if you try to stay comfortable all the time, and avoid anything that feels new or uncomfortable, you'll never do much! Everyone worries about new situations and wonders what's going to happen next. But worrying about worrying, and thinking you can't handle new things, just makes worry bigger and your life smaller.

Me: Right! So the skills I need to be on the backstage crew are...[I started writing fast again]...**expect to be nervous and not know what I'm doing**; ask questions and watch how others do things; let the worry talk be background noise while I learn, instead of putting worry in charge of my projects; take some Calming Breaths whenever I need to; and focus on getting the projects done, because people will be waiting for them.

Shannon: So what about this next question? "What do you already know how to do that might help you reach this goal?" We've never done this before, remember?

Me: Yeah. I know. But I've gone through lots of new experiences lately, and I've learned to focus on what I want to get out of them, rather than focus on the worry that shows up along the way. For example, there was this asparagus situation…[I shot Mom a sort-of-evil look, and then told Shannon about the club meeting, and my asparagus cheese dog. And I told her about Benjamin's uncle. And Elliot—who was hanging around but pretending he wasn't listening—jumped in and told her about the black snake.] You see, after you get through a tough situation, you gotta remember how you did it. Those experiences add up, and they keep you connected to the "I can handle this" thought.

Shannon: So this next one…what do you say to yourself when you start to worry? Well, I guess you say that you can handle it. That you are supposed to feel uncomfortable in this new situation, and that's normal. And you remind yourself that you have a lot to learn, so it's time to get busy watching and learning and hammering!

Me: Exactly. Let me write that down. Next two questions? Yes and double yes. I am willing to feel uncomfortable and uncertain. It's all part of creating a musical, and we're all going through the same process.

Shannon: How are you going to practice, Casey? You can't build sets on your own to see what it's like.

This was true. I thought for a moment. I had been practicing for months, hadn't I? Even though I'd never been on a backstage crew

THE SHOW MUST GO ON!

before, I'd been letting myself get uncomfortable on roller coasters and doctor's offices. I'd been taking Calming Breaths and moving forward. The situation was new, but all of my practicing was adding up.

> *Me*: I think I'll keep doing what I've been doing. When we go to the meeting on Wednesday, I'll think of it as **just another chance to practice**. I'll be a little nervous walking in, and I won't know exactly how it will go and what we're going to do, but I'm going anyway. When worry shows up and does its usual thing, I'll treat it like a familiar voice, but not *at all* like a surprising voice. There. Done. Looks good to me.

The Game Plan

What is your goal?
I want to be a part of the musical because kids who have done it before say it's a blast.

Do you really want this goal?
☐ No, it's not important to me
☑ Yes. I want it, but I'm not sure I can get there.

What skills do you need to reach your goal?
1) expect worry to show up because I've never done this before 2) ask questions and watch how other people do things so I can learn 3) let worry be background noise instead of putting it in charge of my projects, and talk to myself when I'm worried 4) take some Calming Breaths and 5) focus on getting my projects done because people are counting on me.

What do you already know how to do that might help you reach this goal?
I've learned how to focus on what I want, and taking the steps I need to get there. Like eating the asparagus. I remind myself that I can handle new things, because I can managed being uncomfortable.

What do you want to say to yourself when you start to worry?
"I can handle this. I'm supposed to feel uncomfortable in this new situation. I can focus on what I have to do, like watching and hammering. My goal is important to me."

Are you willing to not know exactly how things will turn out?
☐ No! I HAVE to know, or I don't want to do it!
☑ Yes. I might not like it, but I'll use my courage.

Are you willing to feel physically uncomfortable along the way?
☐ No! I HAVE to be calm or I won't do it!
☑ Yes. I might not like it, but I'll use my courage.

What can you do to practice your skills?
I'll go to the meeting on Wednesday, and manage feeling nervous. And I'll keep looking for chances to step into new situations.

Shannon's turn next. Her worries were a bit different than mine, because she was going to be *performing* in front of people. We pulled out a clean form and started moving through it. As she read through all the questions, I could tell she was already figuring out her form after working together on mine. (Geez, having a coach really does speed the process along, doesn't it? Think of all the time and effort I've saved you. Again, you're welcome.)

Me: Okay, Shannon. Do you have a goal?

Shannon: Well, I want to be in the musical. I think it will be fun. And if you're doing it, too, then we can hang out together and stuff. But I have to audition, and you don't. When I think about getting up in front of everybody and singing, my heart starts beating like a drum. What if I turn red? I probably will. With all those older kids looking at me? Casey, this is crazy! I'm not so sure anymore.

[Mom and I looked at each other and smiled, and then nodded in that we-know-it-all kind of way, which I'm guessing was fairly annoying to Shannon.]

Me: That's worry talking, right there. Feel how it just pops up and grabs your attention? Back up. Do you really want this?

Shannon: Yes, yes. I just freak out when I imagine actually *doing* it. But I get it. I want to do it, but I'm not sure yet how I'll be able to handle it.

Me: Great. So you need some skills to get there, right? First, you gotta expect worry to show up, and you need to know how to talk to it. When you audition in front of people—and when it's something that's important to you—it's normal to have nervous feelings. But being scared is different from turning on your alarm system and freaking out, and you have to remind yourself of that.

Mom: Casey, why don't you show Shannon how to do that? I'll be worry talking, and you talk back to me. Shannon, we used to do this all the time when Casey was younger. Saying it out loud really helps when you're first learning these skills. Ready, Casey? [I nodded. Mom dove right in.] Well, I'm not so sure you should audition for the musical. Lots of things could go wrong.

What if you forget the words? Or start to cough? What if you try out and don't get a part at all? That would be so humiliating! Why put yourself through that? [Mom was good. Lots of practice, I'm afraid.]

Me: (being Shannon): Yes, a few things could go wrong. But whenever you try something new, there's some risk. I can't guarantee that everything will go right, but if I put you in charge, I won't even try! You can continue talking to me, but I can handle this. I'll probably feel nervous and excited, maybe even **plain old uncomfortable**, but that doesn't mean I should quit or run away from something fun.

Shannon: Yes, and I've been singing for a long time. I've been in chorus since third grade, and I really love singing. When I think about the recitals I've been in, I can remember how it was **more and more fun every time I performed**. I even did that solo during the winter concert in sixth grade. Why should I let worry get in the way of what I love to do?

Me: Now you've got it! Anything else?

Shannon: Well, I think I focus too much on what other kids might say about me.

Mom: That is a tough one. Pretty normal, too. It just means you want to do well. And, of course, you have no control over what others might say or think. Can you tolerate NOT knowing what other kids will do or say during the auditions? There's going to be a fair amount of uncertainty along the way, from the auditions right through to the performances. Can you handle that, and be uncomfortable at times along the way?

Shannon: I think I can. And right here I'll add "Take Calming Breaths" like you did, Casey. Breathing helps with singing anyway. Give me a few minutes, Casey, and I'll finish this up [which I did,

THE SHOW MUST GO ON!

and Shannon was done by the time I had refilled both our water glasses.]

Me: So, Shannon… I see you wrote "Sing in front of people" as a way to practice your skills. I'm all ears!

The Game Plan

What is your goal?
I want to audition for the musical because it sounds like fun, and Casey and I can hang out together. And I do really love singing!

Do you really want this goal?
☐ No, it's not important to me
☑ Yes. I want it, but I'm not sure I can get there.

What skills do you need to reach your goal?
1) expect to feel nervous when I audition 2) remind myself that feeling nervous is normal, and it's different than setting off my alarm center 3) practice and use Calming Breaths 4) focus on practicing and singing, and 5) think about the fun when I catch myself worrying about what other kids might be thinking

What do you already know how to do that might help you reach this goal?
I've been singing for a long time, and I know that every time I perform, I have fun, and it gets easier. I know how to rehearse, and to get better with practice. I did that solo in sixth grade, too.

What do you want to say to yourself when you start to worry?
"Take some breaths. I feel nervous because I'm doing something new, and that's normal. Singing and performing are fun, but uncertainty is part of show business. I can tolerate not knowing everything."

Are you willing to not know exactly how things will turn out?
☐ No! I HAVE to know, or I don't want to do it!
☑ Yes. I might not like it, but I'll use my courage.

Are you willing to feel physically uncomfortable along the way?
☐ No! I HAVE to be calm or I won't do it!
☑ Yes. I might not like it, but I'll use my courage.

What can you do to practice your skills?
1) Sing in front of people, even if I feel embarrassed. 2) Practice singing while I'm nervous, instead of only singing when I feel totally comfortable (like when I'm by myself in my room!)

At which point Shannon took a deep breath, smiled, and sang a rousing version of "Tomorrow," Broadway style. By the time she finished, we were all singing and laughing.

"Please, Casey," Elliot said, "Promise us you will stay backstage!"

"Yes!" I laughed. "Pinky swear!"

And Then What Happened?

Shannon and I went to the meeting on Wednesday after school. It was a bit chaotic. We stuck close together until they divided us into groups. Shannon went off with the other performers, while I stayed with the backstage crew. I knew a few other kids, and by the end of the meeting, we had a good idea of what we wanted to do. I chose props and scenery.

After that first meeting, I can honestly say the time flew by. We backstagers were so busy building and painting. And finding the right props was like a scavenger hunt. Shannon auditioned and got a medium-sized part. A few solo lines, but mostly singing with other kids. We didn't see each other at practices, but gabbed like crazy about what we were each doing when we hung out on the weekends. All in all, it was a blast, like our friends had promised.

We definitely had some nervous moments when worry showed up. Unexpected events and moments of uncertainty... now that's show business, if you ask me. Just for starters, Shannon did not eat her lunch the day of her audition, and she told me her hands were shaking as she sang. Mrs. Kim, the drama teacher, assigned me to paint detail with two junior boys whom I didn't know at all. I think I talked too much that first afternoon and then worried as I was going to sleep that I made a fool of myself. During dress rehearsal I couldn't find the vase with the fake flowers (it was under the villain's cape) and the buckle on Shannon's shoe broke right in the middle of the second performance (glue guns work wonders backstage). And we loved it!

By the time the show was done (four months after that Monday afternoon in my kitchen), Shannon and I:

1. had made lots of new friends
2. were **really exhausted and really happy**
3. handled all sorts of uncertainty and unexpected events
4. talked to worry more times than we could count (conversations were brief and to the point), and...
5. had misplaced our worksheets somewhere in the middle of all the fun and chaos.

And...I never, ever felt worried or scared again.

Yeah. Right. Good one. After twelve chapters, you're not falling for that.

Even though I know, right now, how to handle my unpredictable life, I'd bet you a million dollars on the spot that **I will be worried and scared and uncomfortable again**. In fact, I'm counting on it. When I learn to drive a car, or travel to another country, or even decide to try cow tongue at a fancy restaurant, I'll feel uncertain. My worry will pop up and try to talk me out of doing something new. And I'll step forward anyway, with a pounding heart and some seriously sweaty palms. Wanna join me? Thought so.

Solving the Worry Puzzle

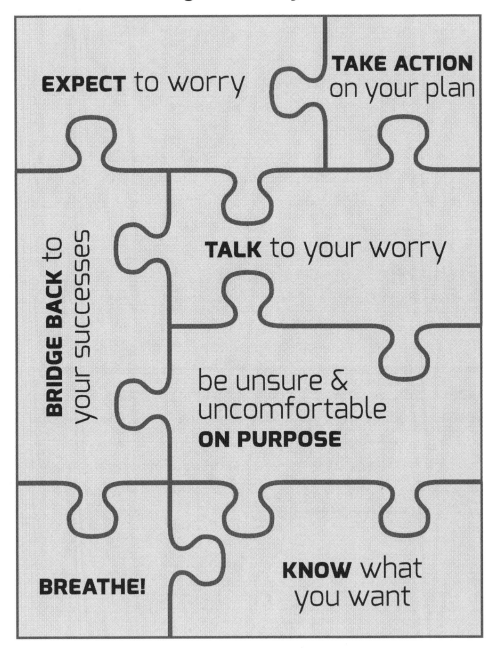

EXPECT to worry

TAKE ACTION on your plan

BRIDGE BACK to your successes

TALK to your worry

be unsure & uncomfortable ON PURPOSE

BREATHE!

KNOW what you want

About the Authors

Reid Wilson, Ph.D, and Lynn Lyons, LICSW are coauthors of *Anxious Kids, Anxious Parents: 7 Ways to Stop the Worry Cycle and Raise Courageous and Independent Children* (HCI Books, 2013).

REID WILSON, Ph.D. is Director of the Anxiety Disorders Treatment Center in Chapel Hill, NC and is Associate Clinical Professor of Psychiatry at the University of North Carolina School of Medicine. Dr. Wilson is an international expert in the treatment of anxiety disorders, with books translated into nine languages. He is author of *Don't Panic: Taking Control of Anxiety Attacks* and *Facing Panic: Self-Help for People with Panic Attacks*, is co-author, with Dr. Edna Foa, of *Stop Obsessing! How to Overcome Your Obsessions and Compulsions* and is co-author of *Achieving Comfortable Flight*, a self-help package for the fearful flier. He designed and served as lead psychologist for American Airlines' first national program for the fearful flier. Dr. Wilson served on the Board of Directors of the Anxiety Disorders Association of America (ADAA) for 12 years. He served as Program Chair of the National Conferences on Anxiety Disorders from 1988-1991. Television appearances: *Oprah Winfrey Show*, *The Katie Show*, *Good Morning America*, CNN, *CNN-Financial Network*, *A&E's Hoarders*, and numerous local news shows nationwide. He has been featured in numerous national magazines, including: *Redbook*, *Self*, *Elle*, *Real Simple*, *Woman's Day*, and *Cosmopolitan*.

LYNN LYONS, LICSW has been a psychotherapist for 23 years, and specializes in the treatment of anxious children and their parents. In addition to her private practice, she is a consultant with several school districts and private schools, helping them to address anxiety in the classroom, school refusal, and social difficulties. Lynn is sponsored by professional organizations and schools, offering workshops to mental health professionals, teachers, school nurses, and parents. She is known for her focus on providing concrete, usable skills. She was featured on *The Katie Show*, talking about childhood anxiety. Lynn received her BA from Williams College in 1987 and her MSW from Boston University in 1990. She lives in Concord, New Hampshire with her husband and two sons.